THE ROADKILL COLLECTION

FLASH FICTION BY JON SINDELL

ISBN: 978-0-9904872-3-4

Printed in the United States of America

Cover Photo: *Roadkill Bunny* by Jon Sindell
Cover Design: Christopher Reilley
Author Cartoon: Judy Clement Wall

BIG TABLE Publishing

Big Table Publishing Company
Boston, MA
bigtablepublishing.com

To my dear wife

Heartfelt thanks to the many kind folks who have supported my work, with special thanks to Eddie Blackman, Chris Bundy, Tony Hecht, Steven Kacsmar, Jeff Kasmer, Leila Rae, Mark Schnapp, and Tony Press for years of encouragement and support. Thanks above all to Robin Stratton for believing in this body of work.

CONTENTS

The author is grateful to the following publications in which these stories appeared:

100 Word Story: "That's Not Love?"
Beatdom: "Hunger for Peace"
Blue Lotus Review: "The Charioteer"
Black Heart Magazine: "Raspberry Jell-O"
Boston Literary Magazine: "Bobbing Heads" & "Cowboy Soul"
Cheap Pop: "The Muffin Man"
Connotation Press: "Crush", "Esther Taulitz", "Soft Spot", "Victory Torch"
    & "The Walker"
Crack The Spine: "My Peace"
Doorknobs & Bodypaint: "Commas in the Right Place", "The Dickens Code",
    "Insidious", "Search Committee" & "A Zinzinnati Red"
Extract(s): "Late Cherries"
Far Enough East: "Banshee"
Feathertale Review: "The New Captain Crunch Commercial"
Firewords Quarterly: "Dhoti"
Foliate Oak: "Damn Sam"
Foundling Review: "One Clear Shot"
Full Of Crow: "Beauty Interference"
Gray Sparrow Journal: "Pop-Up" & "Striving for Perfection"
The Linnet's Wings: "Recession"
Literary Juice: "Don't Like This"
MadHat Lit: "Elmore"
Mojave River Review: "The Driving Instructor" & "The Roadkill Collector"
Nat. Brut: "Butterfly, Brick"
Pithead Chapel: "The Constant Cap"
Postcard Shorts: "Bed Buds", "The Dirtbag at the Gym" & "Hanna-Barbera"
Right Hand Pointing: "Jolly"
Snow Jewel: "Wildly, Wickedly"
Sparkle & Blink: "The Constant Cap" (reprinted)
The Story Shack: "A Swingin' Cat" & "Mud Boy"
Thrice Fiction: "Rabbit and The Professor"
Vine Leaves Literary Journal: "Bobbing Heads"
Writing Without Walls: "The Pugilist Poet Whomps the Big Bag"
Zouch: "Bitter Root" & "The Short, Happy Life of J. Alfred Macomber"

"I wrote a long letter because
I didn't have time to write a short one."
~ Blaise Pascal

MUD BOY

Mud Boy splashed through the puddles and sloshed through the mud, then launched himself onto the soggy turf. The field was so rutted from dog play that he didn't slide but stuck in place–his face submerged in two inches of water, his loins in cold mud. Mud Boy's mother laughed nervously, for people were watching. Mud Boy smiled up with a wet clump of grass sticking out of his mouth. His mom smiled down. "You look like those dinos eating in our book."

"Brachiosaurs!" said Mud Boy. He chomped on the grass and decided to like it. Energized by the boost, he thrashed his limbs as he did when he swam, and Marina leapt nimbly back from the splashes. Mud Boy rolled over and stretched out his limbs, then sloshed about to imprint a mud angel. He howled up at the charcoal-gray sky. That brought curious dogs who barked and pranced and poked at the boy. Mud Boy leapt to his feet and thrust dripping arms skyward: "Let the wild rumpus begin!"

"Don't ever change," murmured Marina, unable to distinguish her tears from the raindrops that clung to her cheek.

Blood Boy loved knives of all kinds, and scissors, razors, scalpels, and pins. When Marina sent him to school with an exemption from frog dissection, he shredded the note with scissors, then smuggled a frog home and dissected it with a stolen scalpel. "These are its guts," he told Mud Boy. The scientific tone of his voice was contrasted by the gleam in his eyes as he scrutinized Mud Boy's face. "Go ahead and scream, Mama's darling." Mud Boy looked down at the tiny string of intestines suspended from Blood Boy's thumb and forefinger like the sausages on the wall at Gladkov's deli. Blood Boy saw his three-years-younger brother's lips quiver, and his hand twitched the scalpel. "Papa hates cry babies," he said, and Mud Boy swallowed hard and replied: "Papa's... not... here anymore." Blood Boy ground his teeth. "Thanks to you."

Blood Boy got *Grand Theft Auto*, a skateboard and spray paint and three secret piercings. Mud Boy got stuffed animals, art supplies, private art lessons, and, at thirteen, a big fluffy dog that he cuddled for hours. Blood Boy got cocaine and a razor blade and urged his brother: "Join me, Sergei. Show us what you're made of." His friend Dmitri sneered: "He's made of mud. There's mud in his pants." Blood Boy's steely gaze willed his brother to comply while defying him to show disapproval. Mud Boy looked helplessly at the rafters and a gang of little black spiders. Blood Boy chopped the cocaine into lines and inhaled fiercely.

Blood Boy got graduation thousands from his absent dad and thousands more from his mom, who could scarcely afford it. He bought a black Civic and muscled it up for street racing. "Serge," he said in a plaintive voice. "Let's go for a ride, man. My car is so cool." Serge sat on the couch wedged between his mother and Poppins, the big yellow Lab. He gave a jerk as if to rise, but Marina squeezed tighter. "Grigor," she said in a voice more tender than it had been in years. "You've got a car and a full tank of gas. You've got money too, and you're handsome and bold! The world is your oyster."

Marina and Grigor locked eyes from across the room. How tall he was, how lean and strong–and his wolf-gray eyes were so like his father's! Grigor gazed at his mother, so lovely and sad, yet peaceful somehow. Her face was weathered, and there were many more gray strands in her hair–and all of them his, she had so often joked. And not joked, too.

"Be free now," he said, and flew from the house.

RASPBERY JELL-O

I was *Laurie* 'til fourth grade when I put on Mom's nightgown. I told my sister, "I feel like a queen, Mercy!" Mercy took the nightgown up over my head and said, "We'll make you feel like a *king* now, Laurie." She got me a king crown and I used Dad's robe for a robe. Then my parents said, "It's time to stop calling you *Laurie*."

I loved girl things but I didn't even know I was doing them 'til I got punched in middle school. Dad said, "Those idiots are trying to teach you a lesson, Lawrence."

My best friends in middle school were almost all girls. I loved Chloe best. She was Goth and skinny from throwing up in the bathroom. We hid in the cave under the low juniper tree in the playground and she showed me how she cut. A little drop came out of her arm like raspberry Jell-o with a star inside from the light that came in. There was a tear in her eye like a diamond, and it just sat there without falling out. She wiped her Exacto knife on a alcohol pad and handed it to me. I cut into my arm and smiled at her, and when she smiled back her tear dropped on the sand.

I'm in tenth grade now, and I love arts and crafts. It's a girl thing, but that's cool with my parents. "Just be yourself," Dad says, and Mom sort of nods. I'm the only boy in the club besides Ronnie, but he's gay. I make chains of cutout people colored like rainbows and stretch them out like a assembly poster we had about tolerance. They told us celebrate diversity and a lot of kids sang, but after school Ronnie got pushed. I took my finger and touched the blood that was on the tree, then I put my arm around his shoulders and kissed his hair.

Abuela left me her rosary beads and a painting of Jesus with blood dripping down from his crown of thorns. I get it out of my treasure chest and stand it up on my desk next to Abuela's picture. I look at Abuela and she smiles at me, and then I cut where the nails go in.

ELMORE

Elmore, twelve, listened to news radio under the covers. Health care mandates and budget battles, hiring freezes and tax reform. A world of magic inside that box.

He mouthed the words like incantations. *Retaliatory tariff. Assault weapons ban.* The deeper he dove, the less he heard his nineteen-year-old sister, who had forsaken him, carousing with her surfer boyfriend, or his mom and "Uncle Chad" shouting and moaning, or clinking bottles and guffawing like fools, or arguing in sharp hissing tones.

Breakfast was at the coffee table. The others hunched over donuts and coffee and old black bananas while Elmore ate bread. The surfer squeezed Belinda's thigh as Chad gazed at the screen. The mother noticed Elmore's strange, private smile. He was growing up–she must help while she could. She cinched her robe, clicked over from a cartoon to the news.

A filibuster on tort reform. "Baby," she said, "what's all that stuff mean?" He shrugged, and she brought out their golden days rhyme: "Tell me more, Elmore!"

How pathetic she looked. As all of them did.

"Well?" she said. They all watched him now.

His smile widened. He knew, yes he did.

But he just wouldn't say.

A SWINGIN' CAT

Danielle Snow was the cleverest girl in eighth grade, a storywriter with a penchant for old-fashioned sayings. She was also the cutest. That year, we had dance parties at kids' houses every Friday night. There were core kids and quorum kids, and I was a quorum kid, there to fill out the room. Mike Freese, handsome and confident, was core.

The final party of the school year was at Danielle's house. Dani was seated on the sofa with boys all around, like Scarlett O'Hara. Her gaze was cast coyly downward at Miss Brontë, the white Himalayan on her lap, as we vied in lame ways to earn her affection. One or another would attempt a witty remark, and she'd pierce every one with a clever riposte. At one point she sighed and wrinkled her nose. "There are more Axe-soaked boys in here than you can shake a stick at."

"I don't think so," said Mike, who grabbed a wooden ruler and shook it at all the boys in a humorous impression of a cranky old man.

Dani served Mike a promising smile. I noted his technique.

Two hours later, with the party waning, and a summer without hope of seeing Dani looming, Dani observed, "You can't swing a cat in here without hitting a Halo fanatic."

"You're right!" I said. Filled with sudden inspiration, I grabbed Miss Brontë by her back legs, yanked her from Dani's lap, and swung her in a wild arc, striking Nick Flores.

Nick's arm took five stitches, and the cat broke its leg. Now who the hell knew that cats' legs were so brittle?

I changed schools next fall.

I was nice-kid cool but Mike Dupree was straight-up bad, so I followed him in pursuit of deep cool. He removed the grill to the crawl space beneath the middle school and climbed in feet-first. In the glow of ten or twelve candles sat a rogue's gallery of the worst kids in school: the unibrow bullies Rafi and Dirk Nimsky, the suspended Marcus Burgess, and Richard Horowitz, who threw firecrackers at cats.

"Wow," I quipped, "welcome to Club Fire Trap."

Their expressions ranged from hostile to blank, but Mike assured them I was cool. "We were just lifting at Walgreen's," he said. "Show 'em, Ziggy."

So I placed the Yu-Gi-Oh! cards I had swiped in my first heist ever on the crate they were using as a card table. They fingered the packs like unimpressed jewelers. "Wow," I said, "it's like the Artful Dodger down here, like that part in *Oliver Twist* when they go through the stolen stuff."

Rafi winced. "You read that?"

"No. A little. We had a test, remember? But I skipped tons." They winced at me as if I stank. "I know it sounds like boring school stuff, but it's a way subversive story about pickpockets in London." The word *pickpockets* seemed to spark mild interest, so I continued. "It was written by the same author-guy who wrote *A Christmas Carol*, which had a great scene about thieves in London meeting in a dark cave or something and trading what they steal."

"You can be our librarian," chortled Richard, and Mike asked me to sit down: "Shut up and sit down," he said.

I'd always wondered what guys like this talked about when they were alone. I sat on a crate and listened while they played poker for cigarettes, but no one spoke for maybe ten minutes. Finally Dirk told me, "You should have swiped some mangas."

"Maybe next time," I said. "Oh dude, it was great. Mike created a diversion by pushing this kid, and I swiped these Yu-Gi-Oh! packs and snuck out."

"You should've swiped something we could sell," sneered Rafi. So Mike reached into his black leather jacket and laid a shiny golden watch on the box. "Twenty bucks," Rafi said with approval.

"Sweet," said Richard.

"For sure," I said. "So what do you guys do down here?" It was a dumb question since I could see what they were doing, but I was sick of the silence.

"We read books," Richard snorted.

"Well it's rad," I said. They turned back to their card game. "This is über ironic," I said, "all this talk about libraries, and we're *under* the library!"

Rafi blew smoke in my face.

"This sure is subversive, doing all these things you can't do in school—like smoking and playing cards—right here *underneath* the damn school!"

Marcus glared at me. "You know, we know you think you're really smart with your big words and all, but we all know that *subversive* means *underground*, so shove it."

"I don't think I'm smart! I hate school. I totally hate algebra and the fascist way they teach history, and the gym teachers are über fascist. I guess English is alright, when you get into Huck Finn and all his wild antics... and that Dickens stuff about thieves is pretty cool." They had all turned away, having clearly decided that I didn't exist.

I sat there in silence. But after fifteen minutes in which the only conversation was a few words about what they would steal next, and Rafi saying, "The new Captain Crunch commercial stinks," I nodded at Mike, who snapped his head towards the exit, and slunk off towards the light.

THE MUFFIN MAN

The Muffin Man had sliced the circumference of his beaten top hat all the way around save for three inches in back that served as a hinge, and he'd flip the lid and pull out a muffin. I wouldn't share because of my weight, but it moved me to think that a poor man would share. I met him with Mom on my first visit to Occupy, one hundred or so pup tents down by the bay. We brought blankets and food, and Mom was my guide. Gregory flipped his "sun roof," and Mom laughed so hard her hair whipped her face. Later she said, "He reminds me of a hippie charmer I knew."

I returned without Mom, with canned beans and soup. Gregory sat at the opening of his tent with his arms wrapped around his hiked-up legs. It made him look small, but he was tall and solid. His smile was so white, and the whites of his eyes were so bright, I guessed he was twenty-seven or so, despite his leathery face.

"It's a lived-in face," he said with an apologetic sort of grin. He pulled an article about income inequality from the band of his top hat. "Lincoln kept legal notes in his hat band," he said. He smiled like this was the coolest fact ever. "Did your Mr. Marvel tell you that?"

Mr. Martin, my revered AP Gov teacher, had not.

"It's tragic," I told Mom at home as we cooked. "Gregory's house was foreclosed by the bank."

"One of those adjustable rate loans, I bet. The banks pushed those like drugs."

"Hell of a way to treat a veteran."

Mom arched her brow in that annoying skeptical way.

On my next visit, Gregory shared canned tomato soup in his tent. He hung pen flashlights and glow sticks, and it looked like a bistro.

I told Mom, "He has PTSD from the war. His nerves are a mess."

She snapped her knife onto the cutting board. "And what makes you think this drug bum is a vet?"

"He told me! God, you're suspicious!"

Gregory wrote poetry about the war and read it to me. I told him his words were like bleeding flesh. He asked me to write a poem called "Bleeding Flesh," and I did, and he loved it.

"Jennifer–that's enough! Don't you see what he's trying to do?"

I thrust my lower lip. Mom knows she can't order me around when I'm wearing my fish face, so she gripped my shoulders. "Jenny," she said. "This person doesn't care about you." She scanned me from my big stupid glasses down to my big belly. "He just thinks you're *available*, hon."

In Gregory's tent, I lay on his shoulder. He smelled like liquid soap and earth. He laid his hand on my belly so gently, I could almost feel a baby in there.

RECESSION

Mom posted 6,542 pictures of me before I was ten. If I picked up a ball or even a fork, the camera was on: "Danny and me—date night!" We'd sip milkshakes and watch for *likes*. At twenty-five, I'd throw my arms up in triumph. Dad would growl, and Mom would shriek, "I'm teaching him counting!" I was eight when Dad left.

At ten years old, my grin was so weak I refused to smile. "What's wrong?" Mom cried. She reached for me, but I jerked away. So she stalked me, sneaking shots of my back. At twelve I gave the camera the finger, and she stormed to the car and we cried it all out.

From then on she only photographed things. I set my RC boat in the lake. The pictures show its voyage in stages. Thirty feet. Sixty. At forty yards it could barely be seen. I imagined I was on it, sailing away.

I'm twenty now, and I sail with my dad. He sits on the edge and watches the water. He doesn't speak and neither do I, we just slice through the water away from the shore.

"Look, let's play off that *morning in America* riff," said Dick. "Like, *Reach for the stars!*"

"In the morning?" Kevin crushed his cigarette, chided Dick with a grin.

"Okay, then. How about, *Seize the day!*"

"*Carpe diem,*" chirped John, the new intern from Georgetown.

"Johnny," grinned Kevin, "these lunch buckets don't speak Latin!"

"*And* they're losing their jobs." Dick's smile brimmed with facetious compassion.

"Nope," smirked Kevin. "They're being *downsized.*"

The intern's eyes darkened.

"Cheer up, Johnny," said Kevin. "We're ministering to lost little lambs."

"*And* giving them a fresh start," said Dick. He squared his hands. "*When one door closes, God opens a window.*"

"Yep," said Kevin. "And we want them jumping *through* that window, Johnny–and seizing new jobs, to steal Dick's phrase."

"*And* avoiding welfare," Dick noted. "Client's politics," he winked at his partner.

His stick-insect arms perched on the huge conference table, John gazed up at the two older men as they paced the room. He admired their sturdy physicality and robust confidence, and pondered the wisdom in brows knit with black humor. He gazed at the sky over the Potomac.

"Listen," Dick told Kevin, "we need to evoke Reagan, the vision to see that a rising tide lifts all boats. And that if a company gets stronger by... *streamlining* its workforce, the economy grows–and all workers gain!"

"By losing their jobs," John mused. His tone was neutral, his affect flat.

"He's a bright one," beamed Kevin, jerking his thumb.

"Yep," said Dick, who ceased pacing to stare down at John. Kevin stared at John too, with a foot on the sill of the wall-to-wall window.

John steepled his fingers, contracted his brow. "I know a phrase." He gathered himself and stared at his fingers with intense concentration. "*Striving for perfection.* The company's striving for the perfect workforce!" He looked up brightly to see how he'd done.

"Perfect!" said Kevin, thunder-clapping his hands. "And the *worker's* striving for the perfect job!"

Dick frowned like an imp. "Not the dead-end sort of job they're stuck in now."

"Nope," grinned Kevin. "When one door closes–" he implied *God* with the spread of his hands.

John smiled like a boy who has just pleased his dad, and Dick, tonsured and comfortably plump, tousled his hair.

Kevin poured a celebratory drink and studied John as he rolled the whiskey around in his mouth. It had been ten years, he had not known the boy personally... but yes, it was he–the altar server at the parish he had long since abandoned. They both had striven for perfection in Christ.

"Yep," said Kevin, smacking his lips and pouring for John. "It's perfect."

Her dad lit his victory cigar with the rolled-up acceptance letter, and her mom was just too pleased to complain. "All those years of hard work," said her mom, clasping her hands as she had through the so-many years of recitals, soccer awards dinners, and speech competitions, "have led you to the Ivy League!" Jessica winced at the stench of cigar.

She fought nervousness with cigarettes her first month at college, used way too much makeup the second, and took up mountain dulcimer in the third, trading writing lessons for music lessons from a waitress who had run from her jealous boyfriend down in West Virginia.

"What about the oboe?" asked her mom with alarm over the phone.

"Whatever, Mom–I got into college, its job is done." Jess raised her Mason jar of blackberry mead to Melissa, and a moon-white smile filled Melissa's round face. Melissa bundled her honey-colored waves into a loose ponytail, set the dulcimer on her lap and filled the room with shimmering notes.

Jessie studied instructional dulcimer videos in the high elevations of stuffed lecture halls and IMd Mel with emoticon hearts to soften her corrections of Mel's countrified grammar. A smug Romeo read over her shoulder. "Jessie and Mel," he said with a provocative grin. "I see like attracts like."

Jessie dissembled. "Yeah we're lezzies, so why don't you buzz off."

Jessie went out for soccer to appease the folks. She was fast enough to keep up with the determined young women with severe ponytails, but slowed to a canter and was cut the first day.

"This is for you," said Mel on a sunny spring morning, handing Jess a letter from the dean along with her tea. "Looks important."

A sly grin crept high as Jessie read the letter of expulsion, and climbed higher still as she rolled it, lit it, and lighted her joint.

RABBIT AND THE PROFESSOR

The Professor shelved cans while Rabbit set cereal the next aisle over. "Hey Rabbit," The Professor yelled at 3 a.m., "will you get me a Coke, please?" The Rabbit raced off on flapping clown feet, raced back stumble bumble with a can of Coke.

Erik, the bullet-headed night crew chief, glared. "Why can't Moe Ron get his own damn Coke?"

"Ah," said The Rabbit, "see, The Professor figured it's much slower shelving cans than boxes, so it's smarter for me to go get it than him. Right, Professor?"

The Professor was hopping to avoid the brown foam gushing over his fist and onto his boots. His abashed smile withered under Erik's reproach: "For the last time, doofus—bean soup don't go in beans."

The Professor slapped his drippy head, clamped beaver teeth to his lower lip. Rabbit whipped off his bandanna and wiped The Professor's apron and hand.

"You guys should gay marry," Eric snickered.

Rabbit's ears burned red, but he didn't speak. Erik bowled away laughing. "I should have popped him," said Rabbit, pounding his fist. The Professor slung his arm around Rabbit. "That's a nice compliment he gave us, Rabbit."

"You're right, Professor. It just means we're good guys."

That weekend, the Night Stockers faced the Day Crew in a Shirts versus Skins full-court hoops grudge match. "Look, we're the good guys!" The Professor told Rabbit. "We're all wearing white."

Rabbit nodded, but his mind and eyes were on Rick Forman: The Needle. The Needle had gone to high school with the pair, but while they were apt to be stock clerks forever, he was a fraternity president on his way to B-school. Rabbit watched The Needle's back muscles ripple as he warmed up with bank shots. "Hey there, Rick," Rabbit murmured sociably. The Needle flashed his old cutting grin, and Rabbit discerned behind the grin the remembrance of the origin of nicknames: the rabbity shaking when Rabbit was bullied, the science teacher who'd dubbed his most hapless student *The Professor*.

"You've crawled out of the darkness," said The Needle.

"Yeah," said Rabbit, "watch out for us night crawlers." He thought the line clever, but wasn't sure why.

The Night Crew held their own for a while. The Professor turned the wrong way, accidentally setting a screen that freed Erik for a basket. "Brilliant, Professor!" Rabbit hollered, sneaking a nervous glance at The Needle. Rabbit's big moment came when he grabbed a loose ball and plodded up the court and laid it in as three Skins overtook him. "Super fast, Rabbit!" The Professor cheered. But when Rabbit started back up the court while glancing at a courtesy clerk he had a crush on, he bounced off The Needle and fell back onto the blacktop. He stared up at The Needle's leer. He thought he should jump up and smash his mean grin, but sat there consoling himself that hey, he wasn't shaking, and that was something.

THE CHARIOTEER

Robert wasn't tall, but had beautiful muscles he'd built in the weight room, ostentatiously squealing with each thrust of the bar. He was fast, too. In intramural flag football during freshman year, he'd fly around end with the flags on his hips fluttering just out of reach of lunging defenders, then streak downfield with his chin tilted up and his torso erect, his hair streaming like a comet's tail. To me he looked like a charioteer. One time I galumphed downfield to congratulate him on a game-winning touchdown. Standing in the warmth of his reflected glory, I told him that he looked like a Roman charioteer charging down the straightaway of the Circus Maximus. We were taking Western Civ–I for love of the subject, he to dispense with a breadth requirement before focusing on his business major–and he smiled as if apprehending the scene. Several times over the next several weeks, he hinted that *Roman* would be a great nickname.

It might have been–and that was the problem: for I disliked the aggressive connotation of the nickname, and was annoyed by his vanity. So I shifted the conversation by noting that Apollo, too, had been a charioteer. Robert misconstrued my observation as the suggestion of a nickname, and his eyes shone with a light like that I had loved back in high school, when we talked about nothing–and everything–during the infrequent moments he carved for his one-time nerd bestie from middle school out of a schedule packed with AP classes, SAT prep courses, track and field practice, and student government meetings. The college-age Robert had long since jettisoned the high school Robert's budding interest in literature, art, and music, but *Apollo* suited him from a physical standpoint, for his limbs were strong and perfectly proportioned, his face was a paragon of balance and proportion, and his gaze was earnest in that school yearbook way. Robert's earnestness had impressed me greatly in high school, for I was much too scared to be earnest. The school put on *The Importance of Being Earnest*. For weeks afterward, I called him *Ernest* and he called me *Ernest*, and inane chuckles always ensued. And when I

28

confessed in the after-school park that I loved him for his earnestness, he said with transparent nonchalance that he wouldn't mind if I made *Ernest* his nickname. His obtuseness annoyed me, and I buried the name.

Standing in the end zone heaving and smiling, Robert gazed at the sun and mouthed: "*Apollo.*" I ignored the hint and suggested beer. Robert's smile collapsed, and he fixed me with a stare suggesting that he had only just now, after all these years, discovered the true treachery of my nature.

"You never do what I want," he declared.

We refrained from contacting each other all summer. And when IM football resumed in the fall, Robert was attended by a woman who stood as erect as a statue, clutching his hand in a proprietary way. The woman was not particularly pretty—not the sort of girl that guys as handsome and ambitious as Robert typically pair up with—but she bore herself in a regal manner. My grandmother would have said she had class. She smiled as I approached, and appraised me with a cool reserve that made me painfully conscious of my underdeveloped body, my gangliness, and the many deficiencies of character manifest in my face. She extended her hand without moving her body, and Robert said, in a half-apologetic yet combative way, that Helen was a business major too.

"I'm an I Don't Know major," I joked.

Helen returned a pitying smile. "Sometimes it takes a little longer to figure things out." She gave my hand an encouraging squeeze.

"Game time," said Robert, and charged across the grass at full speed.

"Robert's quite an athlete," I muttered as my cheeks flooded red.

But Helen was gazing at her future husband, cupping her hands and cheering, "Go, Roman!"

"You're wildly, wickedly funny," he told her.

"I'm 'wildly, wickedly funny,' he told me!"

"Looks like the boy's comin' straight on for you," said Sheila's best girlfriend, rising to do her Nancy Wilson air guitar thing, Sheila rising to rub against her friend's flank. They'd been doing this since high school eighteen years before.

"You're fiendishly funny," he grinned on the second date when she ventured a double entendre that he riposted with a mild innuendo. She felt faint in the glow of his silver-blue eyes and sang, "Devil with the blue eyes! Blue eyes! Blue eyes!" and he smiled with amusement, for he knew the old tune. "You make me think of Paula Poundstone," he told her, and her stomach churned–what if he thought that Paula was plain? Yet she tingled, too, because he thought she was funny–like Paula, *Le Paula*, The Great One, *Le One*.

"Listen," she said in a gruff Poundstone tone, "that's some kinda nerve ya got there buddy, ya better watch out I don't rip my blouse open right here in this restaurant," the words leaping from her lips before good judgment could stop them.

He leaned across, cupped her hands in his.

She lowered her eyes lest he see to her core.

"You're so funny," he told her on the third date, the Bay Bridge lights shimmering in the fog. He turned her from the bridge to face him, pressed her hands to his chest, looked with meaning into her eyes. "There's a sensitivity in funny people that I admire." He paused as if weighing how much to reveal. "I wish I were funny."

"Wish I *were* funny!" She tossed her head back. "Boy, way to rock the old subjunctive mood there, Professor! I'd better watch my grammatical butt around you!"

He frowned at her deflection of his confession. To regroup, he said lightly, "By the way, I'm non-tenured."

"Non-*tenured*! In my family, 'ten year' refers to Uncle Bob's taste in girls!"

He winced, looked skyward in pained contemplation. "What I mean is, there's a certain depth in comedians that I feel I–"

"Don't worry about depth, baby! It's the motion of the ocean, not the length of the sub!" She closed her eyes and lifted her face to his, but all she could feel was cold mist on her lips–for he had lost himself in wonder at the undulating lines of the Bay Bridge light display. The upward-moving lights glowed like–What? He searched his memory–Yes! That was it! They glowed like the translucent silk filaments that dripped from glow worms in caves to ensnare flying insects, he'd seen it on a nature program, hundreds of filaments shimmering in the darkness with their clear beads of mucus, and he smiled within as he determined to visit the natural history museum–tomorrow, after running, but before doing laundry.

THAT'S NOT LOVE?

It was movie night, and the old Jewish milkman was asking his wife if he she loved him after all those years. With singing, of course.

My wife grabbed my hand and squeezed it hard. When the song ended she turned and looked at me like, hey, we're like that too, aren't we? I smiled weakly.

No sex again that night, just toddler time. Then at two I was jolted awake. The shouting came from a neighbor's apartment, all ragged and tender. "God damn it, you fucking bitch–I love you!"

Well, maybe that's it. Christ, who the hell knows.

She was much too thin and her cheeks were drawn, and her ice-blue eyes dominated her face: she looked like a prototypical Russian model, he thought, not a retail clerk. "You're even more beautiful in person!" he gushed, fumbling for her carry-on bag. "I'm Roger."

Her pout was amused but not unkind. "I'm Olya."

"I know!"

He treated her nightly to dining delights: Italian, Korean, Mexican, Indian, fusion, Japanese, Thai, Chinese. She ate with restraint even though underfed, swallowed tiny sips of sizzling rice soup as he leaned forward like a gratified dad. "It's nice," she said, and patted her lips with a delicate movement that swelled his heart. "Are you sure you can afford all this meals?"

He puffed his big body. "Programmers do pretty good here, Olga."

The honeymoon was at a Mexican resort with unlimited foods from many cuisines. She ate delicately. He tried not to gorge. She had put on weight and looked trim in her swimsuit, he hid his belly under a tropical shirt. That night, their first, she assured him that he could not possibly crush her, but he took tender care nonetheless.

"Now is time for Russian food," she told him at home, standing ceremoniously before porcelain bowls decorated with rustic scenes and mounded with eggplant spread and cabbage salad. There was brown bread in a basket and steaming bowls of borsch.

He lowered his head to the dark-red broth, settled some in his spoon, wrinkled his nose at the earthy aroma. He looked up into her hopeful gaze, blew steam, stopped his nose. He sipped and pooled the broth in his mouth. She watched. He swallowed. "Is good?" He sensed the heft of the silver spoon, regarded the gilded bowls he had purchased, considered the expensive dining room set. "Listen, Olga. I just don't like beets."

She sucked in her breath. "Maybe only at first." He inhaled, winced, and laid down the spoon. "Eat bread," she muttered, claiming his bowl.

She served borsch again next week, and next month.

"Olga," he said, "I don't like beets."

After three more years of learning English, she said with brave humor, "Nothing beats beets."

"Olga, listen. I don't like borsch."

She found Russian friends and served it to them. "Olya," they said, "your mother must have been a wonderful cook."

Her mother's death had unchained her from Russia. "It's seasoned with tears. Her tears and mine."

"She was too good for your father," said Irina, who knew of the broken noses of mother and child. "This soup was much too good for him."

"Olga," said Roger after five years. "Enough with the borsch."

"You eat everything else!" She stalked towards the door.

"Olya! Wait!" He slurped and slobbered, poured borsch down his gullet. His wife's borsch overflowed his lips, spilled down his chin and onto the table, soaked his lap. "I'm eating!" he cried. "I'm eating!" he cried like Mama's best boy.

Maggie planted a butterfly garden. Purple coneflowers, clusters of goldenrod, sea-pink asters. I built the hardscape: flagstone deck and brick wall trailing ivy.

I scrutinize Maggie. "Honey. Baby. Why are you mad?"

"Who's mad?"

"You are."

She flips her head. "So you're a mind reader, too?" She zig zags through the garden.

I rush after. "Wait, honey." A thorn pierces my thigh. "What do you mean, *too*?"

She stretches to prune a young branch from the maple. The tree is a sculpture. Her trees are all sculptures.

"What *too*?" I repeat.

She gazes at the tree's delicate limbs; its lacy, leafy fingers.

"Honey," I say. "Tell me. Come on."

She brushes past me and zips towards the house. "I have sauce on."

My head hurts. My ears burn. "What *too*?" I'm chasing. "You're driving me nuts."

Her crooked smile drives me wild in good times, destroys me in bad. "*I'm* driving *you* nuts?" She lowers her eyes, laughs derisively at me.

"What does that mean?" My voice is a life form beyond my control, ascending and shrill. "What does *that* mean, '*I'm* driving *you* nuts?'"

She adds fresh basil without tasting the sauce. The kitchen smells great. She pours cab, swallows hard.

"Maggie," I say, and this is a breach—we always use endearments—but she won't stand still and won't look in my eyes. "What do you mean, '*I'm* driving *you* nuts?'" She flies to the garden. I hustle after. "Honey. Listen." She stands before the lemon tree. Her back is to me. The tree's heavy with fruit. After working the soil, she likes to rub juice on her hands. She makes pink lemonade and ginger-lemon tea. "Listen. You said I'm driving you nuts."

She turns, and the pruning shears gleam in her hand. "No," she says in a hard, quaking voice, "*you* said I drive *you* nuts—"

"Because you wouldn't tell me why you said *too*!"

"What *too*?!" Her voice is louder and shriller than mine. She zips into the depths of the garden.

"*The too*! *That too*! We were standing by the pear tree, and you said, 'So you're a mind reader, too?' Too, what? What too?"

She wheels to go, and there's the brick wall.

CRUSH

At seven years old, Billy Rowan accidentally crushed a snail into a gob of slimy flesh and cracked shell. The sound of the cracking crush plagued his dreams, as did visions of snails advancing on his bed in military-style columns.

He forgot about snails until thirty years later when he bought a small house that his glamorous wife considered a mere stage in their forced march towards a Golden Gate view. The house had a little green-garden that Bill tended with his son, and he sank bowls of beer for the snails to drown in, or dropped them into jars of salt water. Sleeping under the stars on a father-son summer trip to the redwoods–Marie preferred to stay home and shop–Bill's ten-year-old son, Matty, allowed a banana slug to crawl up one side of his face and down the other, and Bill was amazed to see his son giggling, overflowing with joy. Back home at snail-picking time he knelt at the raised romaine bed, set his chin on the soil and studied a bull snail–its glistening, pebbly moist gray flesh, its questing antennae–and before many days passed, resolved to stop killing snails.

He built ramshackle little barricades of mesh and wood, but Marie thought them ugly and yanked them out.

He discovered non-toxic pellets that he presumed were not deadly, but he soon discovered that they caused snails to starve, and he cursed himself and ceased using them further.

He discovered a solution that was simplicity itself, to collect the snails in a paper bag and transport them to a nearby park.

He discovered the courage to quit his managerial job with a company that made meaningless products using harsh labor practices that he supervised.

Marie discovered she could not love a fool. She girded for battle in expensive business clothing designed to make an impression in court and in revealing outfits designed to entice better men than Bill.

Bill knelt to the chard in a cold evening drizzle with a miner's-style light on his forehead, gently dropping snails into a bag for transportation to their new home.

Marie stood behind him beneath a black umbrella, wearing a snug long gray coat over a cream-colored cashmere turtleneck and a red kerchief. Bill swiveled on a rain-soaked knee and blinked up in the darkness. She looked like a model, as she'd been when they met. His eyes asked a question that encompassed all others.

She looked down at him there, on his knees, in the rain, with rusty tongs in one hand and a bag of snails in the other. A snail crawled between them. Marie raised her spiked heel over the shell and crushed it, just for him.

He just couldn't lie, and she loved him for that.

"I love your cowboy soul," she had murmured that first time in bed, and she loved him for not saying "I love you" back.

She loved his crazy passions, his noble defeats, and his hatred of praise.

She loved his clowning as Brandon's Mad Dad.

She loved him for losing all of those jobs without making excuses—for that or their ruin.

But he just couldn't lie.

So she waited for years, until Brandon had fled, and she said at last, with a trembling lip: "It's the bottle or me."

BANSHEE

Her eye wells are black as her irises are as her hair which is stringy and curtains her face which is white and porcelain smooth, and her eyes are as poignant as ten days before when we met at a disjointed party. I was a fringe guest like the eight or ten others who had taken refuge in the cold dim garage from the main party upstairs and did not know the host, a middle-aged, house-painting, drug-debased poet, the friend of our friends, and we all sat transfixed as a stoned, skinny woman, late thirties, cheeks drawn, with a silver winged Mercury helm on her head, played an ethereal riff on a keyboard. The riff was okay, very fast, sort of spacey, the kind you would enjoy for two measures, maybe, assuming, as you would, it would lead to a song, but this led to no song, it just looped on and on, first for moments, then minutes, but no one stopped watching or spoke as she played.

I and two other tekkies in our mid-twenties were too unsure of our place and too earnest in our groping for the San Francisco spirit which had brought us to town to ask her to stop. But the long-timers there sank into the music, a late-fifties man on a moldy old couch who sat with eyes closed and waddled his head, and a white-bearded man and his white-haired woman who sat with vined fingers nodding like the supportive parents of a confused wild child. In a dark corner, a furtive-eyed woman picked at a scab and stared at the dime-sized pool of blood she uncovered.

The woman with black eyes, twenty-seven or so, accounting for sorrow, gazed at the women playing the riff with an expression that mingled respect and compassion. An uninvited couple, in their thirties, insinuated themselves into the garage through the open side door amid fingers of fog. They were dressed in costumes that must have cost hundreds, a samurai and a geisha, and they looked down on us, discerned our orientation, and asserted themselves in the center of the garage facing the woman who was playing the spacey endless riff. The samurai, bulky and bearded, a lawyer perhaps or an investment banker, stood with legs wide in a martial stance, and grinned derisively at the player. The geisha smiled in the samurai's ear, then looked down at me with a testing smile that I rebuffed by jerking my face towards the player to display respect for her. The geisha scanned us, flayed us all with her eyes. "So this is what you do?" she proclaimed caustically. The woman with black eyes extruded a screech as thin and brittle as life escaping, and set tragic eyes on the keyboard player. I crossed before the accusing intruders and knelt to the woman. She lowered her eyes to her white bony fingers and walked them down to the cliff of her knee. My hand swooped down and clasped her fingers; she smiled at the linkage. I searched for something witty to say, some wry, dry remark in the James Bond mold—I was paid to be clever—but the woman saw it coming, and gasped mortified and stopped up my words.

There were no words at my place, just moans and shouts and screams and tears, and the hot searching wind of call and response, and primal murmuring when we reposed.

I spoke in the morning to offer her coffee. She shook her head as if shaking bugs from her hair, hugged her knees with her arms, sunk her chin in her knees and rocked herself soothed. I brought her tea and toast on a guess, and she sipped and nibbled and smiled at me in a soft, wary way.

I spoke at work, and hated my words. She spoke at work, and hated her words. She didn't say this and she didn't need to, I knew it as surely as she knew my body, every thrilled response, every evasion, every insecure juncture of body and mind. We'd throw off our words like our heavy wool coats, and she'd peel the bedding back onto the floor, for we must love exposed, her unspoken decree, and we were vine and tree, and vine and vine, and we squeezed, clung, plunged, probed, dug, dove, and tasted and tried, and she guided me with the pressure of limbs and with primeval sounds, and when I was vain she would screech and withdraw, and I'd clamber back over and nuzzle her neck.

I never turned on the radio, TV, or music, there was only our breathing and moans and giggles and groans and tears, and the sounds of the Mission as we lay like snow angels, listening with eyes closed to kids shouting in Spanglish, car horns, feet running, the wailing of sirens, her mouth forming an O in sympathy with the sirens but no sound escaping. We lay naked, limbs splayed, hands linked, feet touching, and then, when our bodies were pimpled with cold, we turned of one mind and melded our warmth, and clung, pinched, dug, nosed, scratched, stroked, tongued, cried, and dug deep impressions into each other, and pulled buried secrets out of each other.

"Poets of the body," I smile now, on the tenth day, "like Whitman," I smile, thinking myself deep.

She looks at me now with startled black eyes and emits a thin screech, smiles like winter sun, clutches her clothes to her breast and is gone.

BED BUDS

I've got a shoulder bud and a friend of the foot when I lie on my back: the fat tab on my shoulder, the eighty-pound golden pinning my feet. They're strictly don't-invite-'ems, so Samantha, the tabby, occupies the North Country while Bev faces south. We fall asleep like that, and when I awake, they're in the same place.

My son, twenty-five and estranged for four years, chose the tabby fifteen years back; my ex-wife picked the golden. They're soft and warm and smell bakery-good. Samantha licks my hands like a mama cat, and in the morning Bev nuzzles my cheek. I give her two Cheese Bobs from a box on the nightstand, then she lays back down on my feet, as I've taught her, and I give her two more. My reaching jostles Sam, but she's a sweetheart and settles back in. I'm so grateful I bury my face in her fur.

I have snacks of my own on the nightstand, and the laptop's there, too, so I can read the sports without getting up. And I never drink anything after eight at night so I won't have to get up in the morning to pee.

The bed is our island, our magic carpet. Samantha's a slab of concrete on my chest, Bev's a horse on my feet—no way I can get up. Every morning I lie in suspense, wondering when they're gonna move, praying they won't.

Let go of your thoughts, let go of your thoughts, your thoughts are a river passing you by. I'm next to a river watching my thoughts.

Those are heads floating by! Ten or twelve floating heads, what the hell was that saying—if you sit by the river the heads of your enemies will come floating by? That's bull, you should get 'em before they—that horse head scene in *The Godfather* was cool, who the hell was that actor?

Just let it go, Bob. Oh, so many heads floating by, floating, bobbing like apples—who the hell bobs for apples? That's a *Golden Book* thing, *Little Golden Book* thing, who the hell reads that crap? Who the hell brings apples to the teacher, even, even brown nosers don't. *God* I'm fat. *Man* I'm fat. My arms feel fat on the arms of the chair—sweet, wonderful chair, soft and sweet like me, cost me six-hundred bucks—it takes a real man to earn money like—

Breathe, damn it, your blood pressure needs it. Breathe in, breathe out, man, the old man'd cough his lungs out from that, what a fool, dead from smoking—I'm ungrateful to say it, Dad'd whack me for that!

Candy cigarettes were good. All these dumb kids today, we're so over-protective—like Sandi, dear god, just let the kids be! Man, it makes my blood—

Breathe in, man, breathe out. Watch your thoughts float—what's that? Jesus, Sandi, I said keep those kids—

"Quiet out there! I'm effing meditating!"

Breathe in, breathe out, breathe

JOLLY

The new young guy on the block seemed alright at first–not because he was white, but because I could talk to him in English, like when everyone around here was Irish or Italian. Plus he had a wife and kid, which was nice, and he put in a little garden in front, which was also nice, since the Chinese paved over all their gardens for parking. Well, we're out on the street, and I point out this wrinkly old crone with two big plastic bags full of bottles and cans hanging from a stick on her shoulders, poking her nose in someone's recycling can.

"Oh, that's Jia Lei," says the young guy. And I say, "What?" because there's nothing jolly about bums ruining our neighborhood. And he laughs and says her *name* is *Jia Lei*, and spells it out like I'm an idiot–which of course I am, because I work with sheet metal, not computers. "How the hell you know that?" I say. "I asked her," he says. "You mean she speaks English?" "Not really," he says. I give him a hard look for encouraging these human rodents, and then he starts avoiding me–turning his head on the street and everything.

And then he decides to get my goat. This... *Jol-Lee* or whatever is poking her nose in his bin and drops a plastic bottle on the sidewalk... and the damn fool picks it up for her! Like she's the Queen of England. She shows him all her big crooked teeth and starts bowing and cooing like some dumb old cartoon–*those* were racist, I'll tell you that much. Then the sumbitch turns and smiles at me like he's so good and I'm so awful.

This town's going south, and I'm glad I'm getting old. The only place I feel at home now is the Forty Niner Club, or deer hunting up in Mendo. I was deer hunting when I got my idea. Two ideas, actually. The first was to put a deer head in the can for ol' Jolly to find, like in *The Godfather*. But I didn't. What I did do, I took all the shell casings from a deer hunt and set them in a tomato sauce can on top of the bin, just to give her and all the other buggers something to think about. So I'm watching through the blinds, and ol' Jolly comes waddling up and sees the can. First she looks at the casings with her head cocked like a

45

dog, then her face lights up and she fills her ratty old jacket with them—like treasure! Then she steals the rest of my junk.

Here's the payoff. A week later, the old fool's wearing a necklace... made from my casings!

Now, what are you gonna do with people like that?

THE PUGILIST POET WHOMPS THE BIG BAG

We found Head in the yard in full grizzly mode, whomping the heavy bag so hard it shook leaves from the tree. He was stripped to the waist, his torso thickly tufted, and he stalked the bag with hands close to his chest. Head never danced the way some fighters do— "not with that trick knee–ain't no treat"–nor needed he to, he was immovable, and his flanks were protected by a thick layer of muscle plus middle-aged padding. Head's cool gaze followed the big bag's sway like a big gun on a revolving turret. "Sweet science," he growled, then sprang like a cat when the prey sprints for safety, unloading thu-thump! blowing hot gusts of breath and rolling like a seaman, his eight-year-old Scrapple miming every move, Hot Lisa sucking grass atop the old wooden table and staring at Head through narrowed, feral eyes.

"Stress relief," Head huffed, rocking. "Welfare guy says I need it." Thu-thump!–Head glaring with contempt at the recoiling bag. "You want a piece of what you give me, boss?" Thu-thu-thump! the staccato bursts synching with the rat-a-tat-tat of the pneumatic hammer driving nails for the monster addition next door that loomed over and shadowed Head's pocket rental. "Want a piece of *tote that barge?*" Thu–thu-thump! "*Lift that bale?*" Thu-thump! I feared for Head's health in the thick August heat, for he was forty-eight now, and how strong his heart was nobody knew, for he lacked health insurance and never saw a doctor. "You want a piece of *a raise ain't in the budget now, Head?*" Thu-thu-thump! "'*I didn't tell you to go have a kid!*'" Thu-thu-thump! "Now why wasn't I smart enough to think of that!" Thu-thu-thump! "Oh yeah," thu-thu-thump–"I forgot"–thu-thu-thump!–"*I never got a college degree!*" Thu-thu–pow! Head's torso swelled now with each inhalation. "Stress relief!" Thu-thu-thump! "Can you dig it?" Thu-thump! "I *knew* that you could!" Bu–bu-thump! with a combo that rippled the earth.

Head only now turned to me and his son. Sweat matted his chest, his arms dangled tumescently at his sides. "Stress relief," he smiled as sweat coursed down his face.

"*I* wanna do stress relief!" said Scrap.

Head patted Scrap's head with a big red glove. "I'll learn you tomorrow."

Lisa snaked her arms through Head's from behind. "*I'll* learn *you* tonight."

THE DIRTBAG AT THE GYM

The dirtbag at the gym talks too loud and sweats too much. He has hairy arms and stares at the women.

This is the dirtbag at my gym, posts the woman. He talks too loud and sweats too much. He has hairy arms and stares at the women.

Gross! posts a friend.

LOSER, another.

That belly! a third.

Every *like* pings! in the woman's brain.

The woman watches with a critical eye as the dirtbag wipes down an exercise bench. He gestures at it with a grand awkward sweep, smiles and invites her to chat afterwards.

"I've gotta get home."

The dirtbag cups his ear and leans forward. "Sorry? What?"

The dirtbag asked me OUT! posts the woman.

Gross! posts a friend.

LOSER.

What nerve.

The dirtbag sits down to a cold bowl of spaghetti. He twirls it to the size of a lamb's foot and crams it. The phone rings. It's his daughter from college. The call is a rarity. But before he can swallow to express his joy, she tells him his picture is all over Facebook.

He doesn't have Facebook, doesn't hear her alarm.

"That's cool, hon!" he bellows, and smiles at her picture.

DON'T LIKE THIS

The killer had studied the herd for six months. To her horror, she was becoming like them.

In high school she'd hated *The Family Feud*.

Name a fruit.

Apple?

Good answer! She and her friends flicked ice cream at the host's face, three girls in plaid who mainlined Nirvana and lay on their backs with intertwined limbs, sharing rampaging thoughts and tender emotions with one another and nobody else.

Twenty-one years she had floated free, then loneliness brought her down to the herd.

"My beautiful life!"

"My wonderful kids!"

"My fabulous cooking!"

Dutifully she entered the code: like like like like.

Trembling, she made her first post: a raw heart in cupped hands.

137 friends, but no likes.

She posted a tombstone. "R.I.P. Dignity." And another: "R.I.P. Intimacy."

Silence.

She planned her spree then.

"Oh, your life is so great? Then STFU and enjoy it, you braggart!"

"Look, your kids are just kids—no better or worse than anyone else's."

"Who cares what you're cooking! Now inviting someone over, that would be nice."

"Everyone, stop it! We're dying, and ten-thousand "likes" can't change that."

The herd badly injured and flaming with rage, she calmly took aim and unfriended them all.

"This," said Sanders with a lottery grin, "is a Jim Beam day."

"A bowl-game day," winked Brower, filling four glasses.

James, the token academic on the committee, facetiously raised an unruly white brow. "Isn't it customary to drink *after* a contract is signed?"

"Mere formality," grunted Brower, the powerhouse alum. He admired the gold liquid in his glass. "Talent follows Coach Rogers like chicks follow money."

"Rumors, too," said James with a wistful nod at the unmarked gray file. Next to it sat a cheerful red file marked "Contract."

Sanders, the plump and hale Athletic Director, smiled at James. "It's balderdash, James, those rumors of rules violations and what-not. The man has not been found guilty of one single thing."

With bitter petulance, Brower interjected: "He's a proven winner in three conferences!"

"With three confidential separation agreements," said James with the gentle aplomb that had made him the favorite of forty years of English students.

"Mr. James," said the young assistant A.D., "it isn't a crime to be crafty, is it?"

Sanders took up the cue. "He's a tournament bridge champ, Jamesy. Play poker with him, he'll steal your face!"

Brower scowled at Sanders for the ill-advised word.

Sanders hastily raised his glass for a toast, but paused, like the others, to regard James—who looked down with pursed lips at the investigator's file, the contents of which only he had read.

"Read the file," frowned James, and three heads flopped from the fall of the axe.

Louie stroked his smooth crown while all the other men cheered at the screen. Without a doubt, his hair had thinned. He was forty-five, fading. He sipped the Sauvignon blanc he had brought and grinned acidly.

A bulky young man with a round shaved head stared down at Louie. "Forty Fuckin' Niners, huh!"

Louie checked the man's face. It was flushed and demanding. The man's brandished palm required flesh.

"That's right," Louie sighed. "Forty fucking." He set his glass carefully on the side table and raised his palm. The young man slammed his hand into Louie's hand and wrenched Louie's elbow. Louie grimaced, and the man grinned as if he had sacked a QB. The man was Alfonzo, a warehouseman in a blood-red jersey.

Louie took up his wineglass and stared at the screen. He knew what to do. He had had to attend football parties before. He also knew he could not hold his wine. He poured a fourth glass.

"Enjoying?" asked Chris, Louie's old friend, the host, and manager of the warehouse where the other men worked.

"Sure," said Louie. "The spectacle, surely."

"Amazing athletes," Chris prompted.

"Yes, but," said Louie.

Erik, a stocky blond shipping manager in his thirties, turned to Louie. "But what?"

"Well," said Louie, spreading his hands, "it's simply brute force. Just brute force and speed."

"Well," said Erik, "maybe so. But there's skill in there too. Lots of skill." He turned back to the set. Gore bulled up the gut. "That's what I'm talking about!" said Erik, rising to thunder-clap Alfonzo's hand and a bro-row of others. Alfonzo held a hand as large as a face over Louie. Louie brushed the hand with the tips of his fingers.

"Fuck was that?" Alfonzo stared at his defiled hand.

A fourth glass, for Louie, always brought giggles. This time was the same. Alfonzo gave Chris a what-the-fuck? look. Chris smiled apologetically but set his hand upon Louie's shoulder. Louie sipped his wine in the luxurious security of his protected status. "You sure can pick wine," he told himself.

A receiver leapt for a sideline pass, but a defensive back smacked into him and he flew out of bounds before his feet touched. "Damn!" shouted Alfonzo. "No pass interference?" shouted the others. One was Alfonzo's cousin, Ty, a broader, swarthier version of Alfonzo.

Louis tapped Alfonzo on the hip. Alfonzo scowled. "You see what I mean?" said Louie helpfully. "The athletes can't execute their manuevers without unfair interference. Unfairness is baked into the game."

"Fuck he talkin' about?" Alfonzo asked Chris.

Chris fluttered his fingers. "Guy just turned forty-five."

Alfonzo acknowledged the solemnity of the message with a grunt. "Happy birthday," he said in a stony voice.

Louie nodded. "So happy."

The opposing quarterback dropped back to pass but was slammed into as he reached back to throw.

"Hoo yah!" burst Erik.

"You see—" Louie looked up at the large-bodied young men standing before him to decide which to share his insight with; he tapped Alfonzo's waist, for the young man seemed intrigued by his observations; and if he wasn't, that could be even better; "that's what I mean."

Alfonzo grimaced. "What?"

"Yeah," said Erik. "What?"

Louie looked at the two: one white, one not, both reminiscent of the glowering young men who had sat in his classes at City for years, slouching as if showing interest and respect would signal surrender to a conspiracy of the elite. His lip curled with regret and disdain.

"Compare tennis," he said, suddenly conscious of the thinness of his voice, "or baseball, or soccer. Sports where you can't simply slam

53

into the athlete to prevent him from executing his maneuvers. Where you can't interfere with the beauty of the athlete's actions."

"Beauty of the athlete." Alfonzo's tone was disgusted. Ty scrunched his nose as if from a stench.

Louie chuckled at their childish discomfort with male beauty. "When a high diver launches a beautiful dive," he continued, "no one comes flying through the air to knock him off course."

Ty and Alfonzo shook their heads disparagingly, and Erik edged away from Louie on the sofa. They must be picturing sculpted gay divers in tight little trunks, thought Louie.

"I'll put it in more American terms. No one bombs them."

Alfonzo and Erik looked at Chris like linemen awaiting the coach's instructions. Erik had spent parts of one and one-half semesters at City, where several teachers had made him feel dumb. He turned to Louie, breathed beery breath on him:

"Fuck kind of name is *Perreault*, anyway?"

"French fuck."

Erik grinned in solidarity with Alfonzo and Ty, who, though silent, was listening closely.

"French," said Erik, leering as if at a lurid confession.

"*Oui*," said Louie. "French name, like Babar. French rifles for sale—never fired! French faggots. French truffles."

Halftime arrived, someone turned off the sound.

"Socialized medicine!" said Louie. He had been in the States since the age of ten, but his long-lost French accent returned at this moment, and he welcomed it like a wandering friend. "Free healt care for all!"

Chris handed beer bottles to Alfonzo and Ty and the others. "French fries," Chris suggested to lighten the mood.

"*Non*," said Louie. "But gourmet food, *oui*. Note: the French word *gourmet* has a silent *t*. Like *Perreault*." Through a gap in the red phalanx looming over him, Louie glimpsed young women in tight mini-dresses clinking bottles with men in a bar. "French lovers," he said, though he was no lover. "French pastry. Fag pastry. Don't touch it, oh no! French wine. Such swill!"

Someone snorted and jabbed someone else. Beer bottles clinked and beer was gulped down. Four huge guys in red jerseys stood shoulder to shoulder staring down at Louie like the O-Line posing for the pregame TV publicity shot.

"Healty food," Louie said. "very fresh. Ahnd zee French paradox: zey eat zee good cheese, but no wahn ees obese." He dared to peek upward: eight eyes glared down at him. "International treaties," said Louie, jabbing a statesmanlike finger in the air. Suddenly, the young men ceased to exist. Forty-five, he considered. A time to take charge. The ED ad said so! A time to share wisdom. He looked up with a paternal expression. "Do you guys know, they have six weeks paid vacation in France? You have how many, one? Two at most?" The men checked one another's reactions. "In France, they have four months' paid maternity leave. Papa gets time too."

"Do we have to listen to this?" Alfonzo asked Chris.

Chris reached for Louie's wineglass, but Louie clung to it.

"No bombs," Louie said. "No pickup trucks with macho cowboys. No Frenchman Ford tough." He turned to Erik. "Are you Ford tough? Or a cowboy, perhaps?"

"I'm an American," said Erik. "I thought you were too."

"You can take the boy out of France," said Louie, and suddenly he was back in Provence, wearing shorts, traipsing across a wooden bridge that arched over a stream, carrying a basket brimming with leeks and sorrel for the soup that his mother would make to eat with the bread that his father would bring, the three at a little round table set with blue-and-white linen, talking softly, laughing gently, savoring the lemony tang of the sorrel, admiring the deep purple of the lavender bouquet in a tabletop bottle, gazing out at the sunflowers of the kitchen garden and the wildflower spires on the far bank of the stream beyond the garden, and the woods beyond that...

He looked up at the men with no idea how he had come to be sitting beneath four big men draped in red, nor why they and the man

55

seated next to him all tipped their beer bottles over his head poised to pour. Nor did he care, nor comprehend why, when they glared with contempt at his weak pea-sized eyes, the biggest one pursed his lips in a victory smile, and they all clinked bottles, and drained them, and rotated as one to face the TV.

POP-UP

"He was compensating," said the ex. "His daughter needed a dad who was there, not a five-dollar ball. Still," here she twisted the grin she reserved for him only, "it would have been an economical present." She bit her lip as remorse took hold.

*****

"Old Hank," a softball buddy smiled. "Dude was *crazy*. Ran onto the field at an A's game once and dodged security for two minutes maybe."

"Not crazy," said another. "He made five-hundred bucks."

"That's right," said a third, "and fifty was mine. And he took us all to the game with that cash."

They drank in Hank's honor.

*****

"He was a YouTube junkie," said a friend who was not a fan. "He watched it all day."

"Not any old thing," said a friend who liked baseball. "Baseball bloopers were his faves. Like that fan who caught a ball in his beer. And great catches by fans, like that guy who caught a ball while holding his kid. Hell, Hank probably thought he'd get on TV. Or the scoreboard, at least." He lowered his head, but did not drink.

"The ball was hit by Pablo Sandoval," the first friend said helpfully. "He's famous, right? It would have been a collector's item."

"He did love the Panda," the fan friend admitted.

*****

"Even as a boy, he could never take criticism. He never liked the idea of it even." His dad shook his head. "He thought it was unfair

57

how they'd boo a fan who drops a foul ball. He'd say, if they could catch it barehanded, they'd be out on the field instead of the players." Hank's father frowned in contemplation of whether he had been too critical of his son. "Maybe he was afraid of being booed," he murmured.

But it wasn't that, not any of it.

It was just the hypnotic spell of the ball, rising up from the batter's box and arcing through the sky as if it had chosen him alone out of 40,000 fans, looking like the white rubber ball his dad had thrown to him thousands of times on soft summer mornings. He'd chased those pop-ups hour on hour, and sometimes he'd catch them, and sometimes he'd drop them—and when he dropped them, he'd dive to the ground to pick the ball up as if the winning run of the last World Series ever were standing on third and ready to score. He dove like that when the ball brushed his fingers and sank below the third-deck railing.

SOFT SPOT

I had two older brothers so I lost every game... wiffle ball, hoops. When we did WWF, my oldest brother pinned me and the middle one, Joe, slapped my belly until it turned red. They made fun of me when Dad fixed the car and I would grab the wrong part. I put live beetles in Joe's shoes, and he shoved a beetle into my underpants. He said Dad didn't want me. How the hell would he know?

After high school I moved to K.C. and got a job in an auto parts store. I made decent money and fixed up a used car, so I had a nice ride while Joe was still screwing around in college and Matt was paying off student loans. Then I got a job in a body shop and made real good money and bought Royals season tickets with some other guys. My brothers came up and I took them to the game, and they had to keep their mouths shut because I was paying.

I'm a great fan, great. I cheer for the Royals when they do good, and when they screw up, I boo them, loud. It's good for them, and besides, I pay their salaries. But there's this wise-ass behind me, a know-it-all about fifty, who shoots his mouth off the whole damn game. This one game, I'm booing this washed up Martinez for making two errors, and the smart ass and his wife start cheering extra loud when Martinez gets a hit, just to show that they're better than me.

I take my wife to a Saturday game. We have the baby, four months old, her first game ever. And the know-it-all taps me on the shoulder and says in this show-offy dad kind of voice, I hate to interfere, Pop, but the ball can come over here pretty fast–we're fifth row, lower deck–and I thought you might wanna sit on the other side of the baby, between her and the batter, to protect her with your glove, you know? And he stares at Kimmie's head, which is barely bigger than a baseball and all pink and squishy, and he frowns to make it obvious that he's thinking: What if a line drive smashed into her skull? Then, because I'm obviously dumb, he says: I hate to think what might happen if a ball hit your princess in the fonta–... whatever he called it, the soft spot in her skull. Which has zero chance. But my wife takes his side, so we trade seats. And of course, nothing happens.

The next game we go to, I sit with Jen on my right, closest to the batter, and Kimmie on Jen's lap, because that's the way we sit on the couch, and I like it like that. But the jerk behind us is getting ready to say something about a screaming line drive hitting the baby's fonta-whatever, you can feel him getting ready to talk. So I sit up and hunch my shoulders like a bad ass—I can be one, believe me—and the smart ass can tell he'd better keep his mouth shut, and he keeps it shut, and I watch in peace.

A ZINZINNATI RED

Coulda happened to you 'cause it happened to me. A loyal, red-blooded American man.

Who loves his country. You think that I don't? Think this purple heart don't mean anything? That it don't mean a thing that my name's Schmidt, and some of the guys I shot coulda been Schmidt's? Or that I yelled *Damn Krauts* when I shot 'em? Me, a German, from the most German city in the land?

I'm at Crosley Field enjoying the game. Wednesday, my off day. Not many folks there. No score 'til the third, and then Robinson triples. Damn fine nigger, a young guy says. Like he's talking about a race horse, like a horse in the Derby—they come from Kentucky, across the river. Four young guys, drinking Weidemann. I look over for no reason except they got my attention. But I don't hate Negroes. Partly because Hitler hated 'em, and everything Hitler did made me ashamed. So I don't smile back. Strike one against me.

Strike two was the kraut. I'm German, I crave it. I loaded up my dog with the stuff.

Hey, says one idiot, how's your Russian chow, Ivan? Russian. What a dumbkopf. Papa said don't argue with fools. I ignore him.

Hey, says one of 'em. Don't you speak English, Boris? Hey, commie? Another one throws a peanut shell at me.

I tell 'em, forty-five years in America, my family is! My words are coming out in German order because I'm excited. By my people, this city was built! They laugh like hyenas. Damned Russkie, says one. *Russkie*. What morons! Drunk morons.

Listen, I say. The best of everything, in this land you have. Thanks to me, I say. The war, I mean. Just relax. Enjoy the game.

Thanks to him, one says. And spits on the floor.

Then Kluszewski homers. Hooray Reds! I yell.

Hey, says the leader. It's *Redlegs*, you commie. Not *Reds*, you damn pinko.

I forgot, they changed the name—for the Cold War, remember?

I move my seat. I need fresh air, I tell 'em.

The Redlegs beat the Braves.

Lucky me, they're out on the street. Even drunker, and standing apart so I have to walk through 'em. *Hillbillies*, I mutter. Not too loud, but loud enough. They look at each other like that's what they wanted to hear all along. First one guy hits his fist in my cheek, then they all join in. Country boys, pounding me, stomping me on the ground.

I spit out a tooth, and out my blood pours.

Commie red.

THE CONSTANT CAP

I've been pelted with peanuts, bottle caps and bananas, and jolted in the aisle by guys who look innocently skyward but smirk to show that they did mean to do it. In Boston last week I got bumped at the urinal and sprayed the wall. Fortunately my wits and reflexes are still viable at seventy-one, and I was able to redirect the flow where it belonged. This was fortunate, for if I had sprayed the bruiser next to me, I likely would have suffered a beating.

I've had some of those.

It's like this. As the tone-deaf relation of some team official finishes strangling the last note of *The Star Spangled Banner*, I'll announce, in a friendly tone, "Can't fault her–it's such a wickedly hard song to sing." Simple honesty compels a young man nearby to grunt agreement with the contrary old fellow who refused to doff his cap during the *Anthem*. He'll scrutinize me and I'll twinkle back. If I detect a gleam of curiosity, I'll chuckle and say, "A little odd, to make a patriotic ceremony out of a mere ballgame." Most folks shut me down at this point with, "That's my country you're talking about–*sir*," though a glance should suggest that *Sir* has walked this land far longer than they. Others toss off non-sequiturs: "Well, baseball's the classic American game after all." "True," I'll rejoin. "Which is why the compelled observance of a patriotic ritual makes no sense here, in the land of the free." One young man raised his beer to that sentiment in Milwaukee. Two beers later, he told me that his great-grandfather organized brewery workers in the Depression and got his skull cracked.

I told him in a confidential hush that I don't really want to get my skull cracked, but that I don't intend to crawl towards the grave on my belly, either.

The North Side of Chicago was loads of fun. "He's just hiding his baldy!" a Bleacher Bum quipped. So I raised my fedora to reveal the snowy waves that Gloria ran her fingers through for forty-five years 'til I lost her last winter. Loudly I proclaimed: "My young friends from the land of Studs Terkel, I'm not hiding my head or anything else–least of all my beliefs." They were all in fine spirits on that balmy afternoon, so I fired my bullet-points as we bantered through the day:

* It's a deadly dull song.
* It's militaristic.
* Nobody can sing it.
* It cheapens the Anthem to play it at one-hundred-sixty-two ballgames a year.

"And most of all, folks, here's the main thing." A spindly young man with stringy hair and gleaming gray eyes, the sort of guy you'd picture studying advanced physics or founding an anarchist commune, looked up at me with his chin on his fist. "The essence of America, the very reason we love this country–is freedom. Is independence. Is the god damn right NOT to stand for the Anthem at a damn baseball game on a Thursday afternoon against the damn Cardinals of Saint Looey!" For this I received a cloudburst of claps (It's always good form to dump on the Cards).

The South Side? Not ducky. I attended a day game for safety, but a battery whacked my head just the same. Just a double A, fortunately.

In New York's Citi Fields, a literary agent begged me to write a memoir of my Anti-Anthem Ballpark Tour. Yankee Stadium went about as expected. Two huge guys squeezed into the empty seats on either side of me and pressed against me with jovial menace. No problem. My extensive knowledge of Yankee history lulled them by the third inning, and in the sixth, one fell asleep dribbling spittle and beer on my shoulder.

I worked wonders in D.C. A lesbian waitress, an NRA lobbyist, a Democratic congressional staffer from California, and a uniformed Navy vet from Virginia led a chorus of jeers that drowned out my effort to point out the irony of suppressing free speech right here in the nation's capital. "Hey," I proclaimed during the seventh inning stretch, with arms spread wide to accept their acclaim, "you should thank me for bringing you bickering folks together!" This was right after "God Bless America," which I had just condemned as the impetus for the second coerced patriotic display of the day–which, furthermore, compelled allegiance to somebody's god. Liberals and conservatives alike pelted me with foodstuffs, and I left Washington as The Great Unifier.

There are five cities left of the scheduled thirty. Miami is dicey, for I can't figure out how to ensure that I sit among free-thinking migrant Jews from New York and not anti-Castro Cubans. Texas could be fine, for despite their jaw-thrusting patriotism, I think they'll respect my Texas-sized bravado. My chief fear is Atlanta. Listen: Up in Cleveland, the land of the Indians, I got a five-stitch cut in my lower back from a sharp object while penguin-waddling through the concourse after the game. Why? Because I had supplemented my anti-Anthem routine with a rant against their racist icon, the savage Chief Wahoo. But the toleration of bigotry is not in my game-plan—not now—not at this stage of life—not after so many years of letting it slide.

So when they start up with that god damned racist tomahawk chop in Atlanta, I will say my damned piece—yea, right there in Georgia, the starting point of The Trail Of Tears, where the Devil went down.

Robert read his writing from the laptop resting on his stomach:

*Sub Guidelines: You must write like you mean it. You must write like time is an exhaustible resource. You must ask three people who have read legitimate literary writing within the past month to approve your submission before you even think of sending it to us. You **must not** include a third-person bio, because wtf is your story for, ming? If you mention publication credits in your cover letter, your submission will be discarded and we will not buy you lunch. If we like your submission, we will buy you lunch. If you're a lawyer, "like" means "publish," and "buy you lunch" means paying for the burrito of your choice at our favorite taqueria. Yes, we will unclench our tight fists and hand over money for your burrito. And when the register sings, you will be **a professional writer.***

Alida pressed her cheek to Robert's bare chest; he could feel her wry grin rising high.

"Not too harsh?" Robert asked.

"I didn't cough."

"The text, not the weed," though both knew what he meant.

"Should be harsh. We're doing this for Holden." She sat up, placed the Mac on her lap, gazed through big wire frames at the mission statement she'd written. "These words get me hot."

"Steinbeck said writing the perfect sentence gave him almost sexual pleasure."

"Then get ready for foreplay." Her words floated like the dust motes in the afternoon light:

Mission Statement

If you have never issued fake praise for crappy writing in hopes of earning fake praise for yours, this zine is for you.

If your favorite line from Cyrano is, "When I write a line that sings, I pay myself a thousand times," this zine is for you.

And if you have ever wanted to crawl into Holden Caulfield's head and blast these words when Ward Stradlater reduces his writing to comma placement, this zine is for you:

"Ward, look. A true writer possesses powers of observation honed through years of hard work, and powers of description sufficient to convey those observations. A true writer lives in a humble, watchful manner, and has the intelligence to make at least some sense of the turbulent miasma we call human life. A true writer, if she's very good, possesses the capacity to love her characters, or forgive them at least. A true writer is blessed with vast humanity, and, paradoxically, afflicted with a painful awareness of her own limitations. A true writer places commas expertly.

In short Ward up, yours."

Side by side at computers in their rank one-room pad, Frank worked on stories while Ivan wrote code. Frank would place his fingertips on his head, where they'd jiggle, shake, and voom!–his hands would explode in volcanic inspiration, raising his hair into that mad-genius look. Inspired, he'd type a flurry of words; stall out after eight words; and glance shamefaced at Ivan, whose bug-eyed leer at his monitor promised greatness.

"I can't do it!" cried Frank after three months of this, slumping defeated onto his keyboard.

"Don't worry, I am programming genius. You will be author, and I will be tech star."

"But I can't freakin' write!"

"Find story."

Frank nodded at the screen. "Charles Dickens. *Great Expectations*."

Ivan pressed <shift><command><c> and gestured like a white-gloved servant. "Tap the key."

"*High Expectations*," read Frank.

"Read story."

My old man's handle being Earp, *and my first name* Bobby, *all I could say was* Burp *as a tot, and that's what they called me on Telegraph.*

I grokked my old man's name as Earp *cuz that's what it says on the pottery-thing they dumped him out into the Bay from. My sister confirms. She married the dealer. Since I never saw my 'rents at all, or any picture–they thought pictures enslaved their souls–I imagined them as piles of ashes.*"

"Man," said Frank with misty eyes. "You're a genius!"

"No," corrected Ivan, "*you* are genius. Now let's get famous!" and got back to work.

DAMN SAM

I was Sam at birth, and my very first words were "Sam I am," spoken on Mom's lap as she pointed at my favorite book. But as soon as I toddled Dad dubbed me *Champ* for my heroic deeds with a plastic sword. I remained *Champ* in preschool, and the other kids bought it. It was not an exclusive preschool—Dad was overruled on preschool selection by Mom, the lone representative of the egalitarian impulse in our family—and my fellow toddlers absorbed their parents' deference to Dad's money and presence and transferred it to me. I grabbed their toys with little resistance.

I remained *Champ* at my pricey day school—Mom's influence had faded along with her health and the marriage—and the kids were too gentle to challenge the name. "Pampered princes," Dad called those kids, holding his hands up as targets for huge boxing gloves that swallowed my hands. I strutted around school with my chest thrust out and my head erect, as my father did when he roamed his office like a Roman senator with his striated hair that looked carved from white marble. Other kids at Prentiss had nicknames too. There was Robert Wilson, a jaundiced, bloated kid we called *SpongeBob*, and *Twist*, a skinny little full-scholarship case whose real name was Oliver, who was taunted by the important boys for his sunken eyes and drawn cheeks and the sandwiches of food-bank tuna that he ate every day.

When I was thirteen, Twist and SpongeBob and I walked over to an ice cream parlor on Fillmore near the housing projects. We were under the supervision of an English teacher with wild frizzy hair and a heavy gray coat who felt it would broaden our outlook to mix with all types. I bought a mint chocolate chip cone for myself and a strawberry cone for Twist, who rewarded me with his usual monkey–hopping "Thanks, Champ!" routine. We took our cones to a park across the street while our teacher wrote poetry on a bench sufficiently distant to promote our independence. A group of five or six boys a little older than us were lounging on a concrete wall nearby, and Twist said, much too loudly, "How's your cone, Champ?"

The tallest kid hopped off the wall. "Is that your cone, Champ?"

"It's in my hands," I said with a too-smart smile.

"Ooo!" said another. "He dissed you, Darnell!"

"No, he didn't. Champ wouldn't diss me. Champ's a champ! Right, Champ?"

"Chump," said a voice to my left and behind me.

"Can I see your cone?" said Darnell. Another boy said, "Can I see your wallet." They had sliced through the gap between SpongeBob and Twist and were leaning in from every side. I half raised my hands as my father had taught me, but these kids were street tough, not marshmallow kids like the ones in my school—and, besides, I was holding a cone. "Ooo," said one guy, "the champ wants to fight! Hey there, Champ, show us what you got!" A guy tapped the back of my head, and I turned, and he grinned at me, and I turned back around to the one called Darnell, and he punched my mouth. Our teacher came clomping over in her chunky shoes, and the boys scattered like birds as blood from my mouth dripped onto my shirt and onto ice cream I'd lost to the ground.

The next day at school, Twist said, "How are you, Champ?" with annoying pity in saucer-sized eyes. "Don't ever call me that!" I said, and punched him in the shoulder. He never did again, nor did anyone else.

The teacher was fired at my father's behest.

I withdrew into schoolwork and discovered biology. "I want to be a doctor," I told Dad. He frowned contemplatively. "A fine field," he said in the tone he used when appraising a business deal. "Very lucrative, especially in the specialties." He looked at me. "And of course, helping people." He bought me a legit first aid kit, and when his girlfriend cut her finger slicing premium tuna for sashimi, he insisted that I dress the wound. She rested her slender hand on the marble counter top, and I stuck my tongue out the side of my mouth, cleaned the wound, applied a gauze pad and secured it with tape. Dad appraised my work. "Not bad, *Doc*." His girlfriend, Christine, a tall, slender, pretty young Chinese women from his office, picked up the

70

cue and said, "Thank you, *Doc*," with a smile that I see in recall as guardedly mocking.

I stayed *Doc* until eleventh grade, when a paid college counselor sat down with my dad and Christine, who was now my stepmom. Having considered my transcript and aptitude tests, and my years of lessons with private tutors, he had determined, he said with a philosophic chuckle, that medicine "might not be the best path for our young friend."

"But–" I said, stunned.

"Then what is?" asked my dad, his fingers intertwined with my stepmother's fingers.

"He's good with numbers," the counselor said, a conclusion that could only have been based on a myopic reading of my transcript.

Dad took me to his eighteenth-floor office. Christine, who had been Dad's secretary and was now his right hand, brought in glasses and ice and said, "I'll leave you men alone." Dad poured one finger of whiskey for me and three for himself. "To the future," he said. The drink burned my throat but I told Dad I liked it. Dad stood before the floor-to-ceiling window and pointed to properties that he owned a piece of. "See that office building?" he said. "And those luxury apartments out by the water? Those were all built by numbers. Amortization. Prime rate. Capital gains. Tax basis and triple net rent." He raised his glass to me. "But there's only one number that counts." He appraised me narrowly. "That number is one. One–like *Ace*." He winked at *Ace*, and clinked *Ace*'s glass.

With extra tutoring and post-midnight hours I managed to earn a low B in calculus. I was legacied into the Ivy League, then Dad bought my way into business school, then brought me back home to learn real estate development at the feet of the master. Like my father I dated my secretary, a beauty who gave flattering nicknames to "her private possession:" *Iron Man. Redwood. Joystick. Big Boy.* I bought her a Big Boy diamond in Carmel on a whim, and we took a honeymoon cruise to Mexico. The moon was so bright off Puerto Vallarta that we could see dolphins leaping in channels of moonlight.

I'm forty-four and bald now, with high blood pressure. We have evictions, deals, firings, audits, lawyers, meetings, and mountains of money. I eat due to stress, and pouches of fat surround my eyes. Hard–driving men who have made it on their own, lean, hard–jawed, ambitious, aggressive, see weakness in my eyes and grin with contempt.

Karina, Karina, my beautiful wife, pretends she's asleep when I reach for her waist. She has done this for years. There's a vibrator in her lingerie drawer, and she wears scooped-back gowns to the opera and smiles at men when she thinks I'm not looking. But we've got a pre-nup, so she's not going anywhere with our son.

Dad lingers with a dying liver, a full head of hair that mocks my baldness, a still-lean jaw that mocks my weak chin, and an appraising eye that refuses to see the defeat in my eyes.

"Ace," he says, and frowns at the Bushmills 21-year old in his glass. "Whiskey's cut my life short. Are you listening, Ace?"

"I'm *Sam*," I say. "God damn Sam I am."

MY PEACE

"Hey, Johnny." It was my father, the best man I know. The wisest man, too. Guys at work call him *Buddha* for his bald little head and this little smile that says he knows something that no one else knows. I'm not wise like him and I hardly ever smile, 'cause it feels like something slimy's crawling across my face when I do, 'cause I'm thirteen and weird in a teenage sort of way—too skinny and tall, with a shaky voice and a dumb overbite, and the girls laugh at me, and there's rich poser kids and a moron who pushes me in the hall. Dad always listens nice and quiet when I complain, then he snaps the top off a beer can and says, "SNAFU, Johnny. Situation normal—dot dot dot."

No cursing for Dad.

He's a wise man, a wizard. No matter what happens—more yelling by mom, more crap from his boss—he takes it in stride, with a little Buddha smile like he's millions of miles away and at peace with the world.

I was in the doorway of The Sanctuary, and he waved me over to the worktable. "Did you ever wonder what true peace is like, son?"

I gave him that slimy grin to make him happy, but I couldn't look straight into his eyes—they're too bright and intense, full of super cosmic intelligence or something. Dad doesn't mind. He never tells me, Look me in the eye! like a teacher I know. So he just said, "Let's talk, John," with a friendly voice and a twinkly smile like the dads in the movies, those old black and whites. He's my own movie dad. And he knows real life, not the bookworm crap they feed you in school. I smiled full out. Only my dad makes my smile feel good.

The Sanctuary is our garage, and Dad loves it. He's got a little fridge full of beers for him and soda for me that he keeps locked, he keeps everything locked 'cause he's such a great dad—first-aid, safe driving, all that. He's got a bench and a barbell—he's small, but you can see how pumped he is in the arms and chest when he wears a tee shirt—and he's got a work table where he fixes broken lamps and stuff while listening to football or sports talk or politics. Once we rented

Hunchback Of Notre Dame, the black-and-white one, and when we went to the garage to get away from the drama in the house he said "Sanctuary!" in The Hunchback's weird voice. It's been The Sanctuary ever since.

"Thirteen's a special age, Johnny. You're becoming a man."

I felt my smile go slimy 'cause I knew he was lying.

"Do you know what happens when a Jewish boy turns thirteen? It's a rite of passage, and they call him a man. Did you know that?"

"It's called a bar something." The only Jewish person I knew was my math teacher, and he made me feel dumb with this look on his face that was supposed to be friendly, but really he was laughing at you.

"But John," he said, pointing at his head, "they don't know." He winked at me like he had a great secret to tell from ancient times or the edge of space. Then he put his hand under my chin and lifted it up so that I had to look him in the eyes. His smile got bigger, and I smiled back just like him. "Do you ever wonder about absolute peace?" he said. It sounded like church talk, except we never go. "Do you ever wonder about absolute quiet?" I didn't understand, but his smile was so nice that I kept looking at him. "You've heard the expression *peace and quiet*, right, son?"

I nodded. Dad has this way of pulling me along when we talk. He absolutely should have been a teacher. He's ten times smarter than the real teachers.

"Remember how peaceful it was in the woods last summer?"

I nodded. Last summer we went camping, just us two, and sat by the river just listening to the water for hours, not talking at all. I'm not exaggerating. We did not talk for hours.

"You can have that same kind of peace right here in the city. You can have the quiet that brings the peace."

He reached into his pocket for his big key ring that had about fifteen keys and found the one that unlocked the drawer beneath the worktable. I thought maybe he was hiding a bottle of Jack Daniels in there and would let me have a sip, a rite of passage like a Jewish kid having wine at his bar thing. Or maybe he'd initiate me into smoking grass with his medical marijuana, or maybe he had some Buddhist prayer beads or something.

"Son," he said. "Put your hand out, palm up. And close your eyes." I did what he said. "Now feel that, son."

It felt so good, so cool in my hand. So heavy and smooth. Dad closed my hand around the grip, which had a nice pebbly feel, and slipped my finger through the trigger guard and set it on the trigger. "You can open 'em now."

He was holding my hand in both of his hands with the barrel of the gun pointed at the floor. The gun wasn't loaded, but he told me in a very serious way to never point a gun at a living person even if you're sure it's unloaded.

"Now Johnny," he said. "Did you ever feel total command? Did you ever have the feeling of making the entire world stand still, like it's at your command?"

It was a silly question, so I ignored it. But like I said, he should've been a teacher, because he's always a step ahead of my thinking, always pulling me along until I realize that I know stuff that I didn't know that I knew 'til he shows me.

"John, think. Did you ever feel like you're–" he stopped and gave me this epic wise man look that went deep inside of me, and lowered his voice like a movie trailer guy– "master of the universe?"

"Yeah!" I said. My favorite game.

"And that part where you finally corner Dreyghon, and he puts down his weapon and gets on his knees and begs you not to kill him? And you put your gun right to his head and just... listen?"

"Yeah," I said.

"You know that feeling you get? Of absolute peace?"

"Yeah," I said. I played that part over and over just to see Dreyghon shut his big fat ugly fish face for once.

Dad mussed up my hair. It was funny that he had to reach up to do it.

"Imagination is the key to finding peace, to escaping the aggravation of the world. Did you know they did studies that if you

75

imagine a thing, you feel the thing? And the thing becomes real in your mind, the way your neurons fire and everything?" I nodded, more with excitement than understanding. "They've done studies on these Buddhist swamis that astral project–you know, leave their bodies, transport themselves across a river or something. They put electrodes on their brains, and you can see their bodies still sitting there, but their brain waves are going crazy, like they're really flying. Or they make themselves feel fire or ice even if there isn't any. Like hypnotism, sort of. See what I mean?"

"Yeah," I said.

"Great! So that's what we're doing. Now listen, Johnny. I want you to picture someone who chaps your hide, like that smart ass math teacher, or some stuck-up chick, or that SOB bully. Okay?"

We have a dart board on a wall in The Sanctuary. Dad pulled a picture of a black shadow of a human head from the gun drawer, a silhouette, and pinned it to the dart board. "Alright now. Who's your target?"

I smiled up at him like I couldn't believe I could do this. He read my mind and nodded that I could, and I started thinking of people, but there were so many to choose from that I couldn't decide.

"Well," he said, 'cause he really can read my mind, "there was that big mouth animal rights activist who stuck that flyer in our face when we were trying to enjoy our ribs in peace." Yeah, she was a jerk. "Or those gun control nuts who go on TV every time some fool goes off and gives us all a bad name. You'll settle on someone. Just meditate on it."

So I closed my eyes with the gun in both hands and the barrel pointed at the floor with Dad's hand on my hands, and meditated with the biggest smile ever. Then I opened my eyes and lifted the gun to the dart board.

"Got someone in mind? Excellent. Now I want you to imagine them chapping your hide with their stupid words, like that math teacher or those rich snots, or that punk shoving you in the hall. It's all good."

"I got it," I said.

"Alright," he said. "Now just lift the piece up nice and steady and press it to their forehead."

I pressed the gun to the math teacher's head.

"Now listen," Dad said.

I listened.

"What do you hear?"

"Nothing," I answered. "He like, totally stopped talking."

"Darn right," said Dad.

"It's just quiet," I said.

He smiled as if I was super bright.

He took the gun from me and locked it in the gun drawer.

I don't have the key, and Dad won't get me my own piece until I'm eighteen, but I visit The Sanctuary with Dad whenever someone chaps me, and I find my peace there.

THE SHORT, HAPPY LIFE OF J. ALFRED MACOMBER

Sequoia National Park a little before sunset, little strength in my hand. A nubby pencil I pray won't break.

Prologue

A poem:

Here sits Alfred Macomber, leaning on a tree, d–y–i–n–g.

A prayer:

If I should die before I wake... a bear ate me! haha

Or that mountain lion.

These are my dying tweets. Old-school tweets–on paper. The dying tweets of a Twitter-sized life.

I sit against a giant sequoia, far, far from the trail. A wise old tree, Colonel Mustard I call him. He'll hear my poem.

The Death Song of J. Alfred Prufrock

Wait–

The Death Song of J. Dylan Thomas!

"Rage, rage against the dying of the light!"

How can I rage when I can't even stand?

Note to self: Exclamation points are <u>exhausting</u>.

The Bucket List Of J. Alfred Prufrock

* Take one last tour around the glade.

* Learn to speak owl.

* Admire the delicacy of this fern until the sun sets, then do it again when the sun rises. I hope.

* Meet each star by name.

The Regrets of J. Alfred Prufrock

Not following Matt and Nick into the school that Saturday when I was eleven and the door was unlocked and they ran through the halls and ate in the cafe.

Not following Matt and Chuck onto the roof of the Press's' house, or anywhere else.

Not staying funny after people said to quit the dumb jokes.

Not writing poetry after middle school, or ever reading a poem to a girl.

Not going away to college.

Not leaving my cube.

Not boldly going where no man had ever gone before.

Until eight days ago, when I followed the most beautiful thing I have ever seen, a spotted fawn bounding through the brush and up a steep slope.

Things I don't regret

Staring at a mountain lion who stared back at me with deep understanding.

Observing an ant and its precision actions with microscope eyes.

Letting a banana slug rest on my cheek like a good friend.

Watching a little yellow flower open up every morning to drink the dew.

Seeing that same deer walk into the glade like a ballerina a few days later, seeing her blinking at me and then munching on leaves like my dinner companion before bounding off again.

Plunging my gaze up into a cold black sky of ten-thousand stars.

Living under those stars.

Dying under them.

Joining them.

LATE CHERRIES

My funeral was literally out of the box. The kids were stunned, but they're the stiffs. "You can't do that!" they said with voices mingling their childhood petulance with their current middle-aged bossiness. "Well children," I said, "this paper is my will, and it says I can. So buck up, buckaroos, and have a good time!" So they and the grandkids hiked into the woods, fed my "ash" to a redwood, and danced round the tree, as the will instructed, to flute music by Kaz–or "your friend," as they'd called him for twenty-one years. And so my children danced on my grave, which I considered a lovely triumph.

I should regret, I suppose, that the best years of my life were from sixty-eight through eighty-nine–but what sweet, peaceful years they were! Kazuo and I built a little stream in my backyard with mossy banks and an arched cedar foot-bridge, and we sat beneath the great drooping willow that I had planted forty years earlier, sipping cold drinks in summer and hot tea in winter, and listening to the bubbling stream. Many mornings I painted watercolors while Kaz gardened, or wrote poetry while he played bamboo flute. Kazuo opened my eyes to all kinds of wonders. "My family put the *fun* in funeral," he winked one spring day eighteen years before my own funeral, just before laying his mother's ashes into a planting hole he dug by the Russian River for a cherry-tree sapling. Then we enjoyed his homemade cherry pie.

That was five years after Henry passed. I lost my best childhood friend and a few others I knew at about the same time, and with each death I thought: "I've outlived another. I'm doing well."

Henry's funeral was conventional, and I was proud of how it came off. "You look wonderful," my big sister told me, clasping my hands and probing my eyes for weakness. "And what a marvelous spread you've made!" I shouldn't have smiled, but I was only sixty-six then and still craved Ellie's approval. Besides, it really was a great spread, with my "famous fried chicken" (I still allowed people to call it that), three salads, and my blue-ribbon pies. When I laid the spread out I heard Henry's praise. But that night alone, I bit my lip so hard it bled when I thought about the terrible job I had done for my husband. If only I had read more about healthy cooking, if only I had made him accompany me on walks. If only I had shared my body more often.

Even so, he knew what his weight and his drinking would do, for his knowledge of the actuarial tables was legendary in his insurance company—and, besides, he was just plain smart. And he appreciated my smarts. Our conversations were generally four-fifths Henry and one fifth of gin, "with a dash of Linda," Henry would say. And when he'd finish a lengthy discussion of Cold War politics or the national debt, he'd say, "You're a pretty bright girl, you know that kid?" I'd think about such compliments when fixing my hair before our night out, and my gaze would sometimes drop into the past—before I took a job after the kids left for college and earned three Secretary Of The Month plaques in a two-year period... before a dreamy Mother's Day when the kids served breakfast in bed, with coffee in the World's Greatest Mommy mug Becky made in church... before I painted baby-blue the kitchen shelves that would lodge a collection of Best Mommy mugs... before I left college in sophomore year to marry Henry, who had distinguished himself in the Quartermaster Corps and established himself, in my father's eyes, as a "real go-getter"... before I'd settled on Henry for his pleasant, honest face, his intelligence and his excellent manners—to a warm spring morning when I was eighteen, and was tidying my "honors alcove," as Mom called it, a nook in my room where we kept my succession of horsemanship trophies and Girl Scout badges and citizenship medals, and a scrapbook in which Mom pasted a series of perfect report cards along with my certificates of perfect attendance. I was polishing a loving cup when the nurseryman's son caught my eye beneath my second-story window, and I finished my work hastily and scampered downstairs. I smiled at the nurseryman, Mr. Watanabe, who was unloading Gravenstein rootstocks, and found Mas in the back orchard kneeling over a planting hole, his face broad sunshine and burnished copper. I helped him mound soil and manure in the hole, and he invited me to help lower the root ball. We backfilled the hole and patted down the soil. Then at last, after months of waiting, Mas took my hand. I lowered my eyes lest my love for him burst and destroy the world.

Father saw, and severed business relations with Mr. Watanabe that day. He explained to me, of course, why it had to be done. A few months later, after Pearl Harbor, he explained that Mas and his family had been sent to Tule Lake for their own good and the good of the country. "You know I'm right, don't you, sweetheart?" I averted my eyes from the gaze of the man I loved so deeply and had never disappointed. I couldn't imagine disappointing him now.

"I know," I whispered, and lowered my face as I so often would when I knelt by the tree that my love and I had planted on that warm spring day.

"That's a good girl," said my father, and he stopped and patted my hand into place.

DHOTI

Dad's eightieth birthday was a costume party. I was Maria Von Trapp, my sister hid her annoyance behind Jackie O shades, and Dad's stooped wife, April, wore a burnished-orange sari and a third eye.

Dad was Ghandi, and it wasn't a stretch. His limbs were sticks, for he had cut down to just one meal a day since leaving the university three years before; his head was naturally egg-shaped and bald; his incisive eyes twinkled behind round wire-frames; and his chest showed snowy through his... uh...

"Dhoti, daughter."

I knew it, and Frannie knew it, but neither would risk mispronouncing the word for fear of being cut by a grin for our academic underachievement.

"It looks good on you, Father," Frannie said flatly. She had discarded *Dad* several decades ago and knew that *Father* vexed. But it didn't today. "Thank you, Frannie," said Dad in a benedictory tone. He dipped his finger in the water-bowl—we were scooping April's runny dal with banana leaves—and anointed Fran's forehead. She choked off a laugh and gaped in shock. Dad lowered his head with a soft inward chuckle.

The next day, my father was Gandhi again. He was Gandhi next week, next month, and next year—all day, every day. Frannie and I drove by and saw Dad outside in his dhoti, sauntering in a weak-legged way to the corner market for lentils and peas. "He's demented," said Frannie with bite, but I noticed myself unconsciously mirroring the grin Dad bestowed on fellow walkers.

Dad was still Gandhi when April died, and soon "nursing home" and "his own good" were Frannie's constant themes. So we sat down with Dad in the light that streamed into his study, illuminating the books he had loved for so long behind a door he had rarely opened to us. These days he merely caressed their covers.

I was the younger, favored child. "Dad," I said. He offered a birdlike hand and I took it. He beamed and offered his free hand to

Frannie, but she turned with a pretense of not having noticed. "Dad," I repeated. Dad smiled with wonder, innocence, and grace. Frannie considered this childlike affect further proof of dementia, but I discerned wit deep inside his eyes. And his smile at last was mockery free.

"I can't," I told Frannie. "There are some things you don't do to a mahatma."

ESTHER TAULITZ

The eighteenth person on my list, working up, is a girl from way back in my fourth-grade class, Esther Taulitz—"Toilets," she was called. She was gangly and awkward, with a sallow face with splotchy red cheeks, and black horn-rimmed glasses that made her look like a male accountant. She got straight As, too. Worst of all, she cried in class.

I spoke to Esther just once in school. It was at culmination, when kids were trotted out before our parents to show our stuff. Most kids performed skits or sang in groups, but a few bright lights were featured in solos. Esther had been selected to recite "The Road Not Taken," and I sat on the floor nearby trying desperately to finish memorizing "I Heard A Fly Buzz When I Died," an Emily Dickinson poem that I did not like and could not get, but which Mrs. Jansen ordered me to recite to show off her success with a student who had only just recently shown his first glimmer of wit. Acid burned my throat.

My mom stood in the back of the room in an emerald-green dress with a rust-red scarf pinned by a gold brooch. Her hair had been freshly styled and her make-up was impeccable, though it failed to mask the sadness from her recent divorce. I think there was shame from the divorce, too, because divorce was rare in those days, and every other mother in the room was paired with a dad. But Mom stood tall and straight. I thought she looked brave.

Esther stood tall and straight in the front of the room. Her pride annoyed me, for what right did she have to be proud? She recited the first verse in an extra loud, grating voice, remembering Mrs. Jansen's command to "Project!" To my disappointment she nailed the second verse, too, remembering lines she had struggled with all week. It sickened me when she flashed a triumphant "Aren't I great!" smile at her family in the back of the room. Her mom, dad, and brother, who resembled Esther right down to the glasses, confirmed her assessment with broad matching smiles.

Esther continued:

"Yet knowing how way leads on to way,

I doubted if I should—"

"—ever have friends!" I cut in, loudly enough for Esther and the kids near us to hear.

Kids laughed, Esther froze. Her face flushed. Tears welled. She tried to remember the words but couldn't, and then she imploded and sank to the floor, and lay sobbing in a heap in her brand-new dress. She wouldn't get up. Finally Mrs. Jansen—unkindly, I felt—grabbed her arms and dragged her away.

Forty years later, I've found Esther on Facebook, and now I can apologize at last.

Fifty-eight apologies behind me, with seventeen ahead after Esther, on the farewell tour of a dying schmuck.

THE ROADKILL COLLECTOR

The roadkill collector had soft hands at first, but the wind and the sun toughened his skin as the gripping and lifting strengthened his back. On quiet days he would park the pickup and patrol miles-long stretches of woodland highway by foot. His fifty-six-year-old belly shrunk and his lung-power increased, but he only spoke when spoken to.

"Remember to cook that to at least one-hundred-eighty degrees to avoid trichinosis," he'd tell scavengers. The absence of a smile did not mean that the collector begrudged hungry people a free meal–to the contrary, he was happy for them, and pleased they fed on lean meat. He simply never smiled on the job. He smiled in the cabin when his woman would sing "Roadkill Collector" like "Daydream Believer," but the smile was subdued, and nothing like the aggressive grin of his big city days.

The roadkill collector did not feel compelled to tell people of the wealth he'd enjoyed before leaving the city, nor did he anger when passing teens would yell Loser! at him as he knelt to a skunk. The collector had been known as "The Skunk" by opposing lawyers, and as "The Stiletto" by his admirers at the firm for an eviscerating tongue.

The roadkill collector removed scraps of food tossed onto the roadway by passing motorists lest they lure animals to their doom, and cut sections out of fences to create escape routes for frantic trapped creatures. He collapsed to his knees as if shot in the gut when a man aimed his pickup at a turtle and crushed it, then gathered himself and swept flesh, shell, and slime into a dustpan and buried it twenty feet from the road. He could not speak for days.

The roadkill collector studied Buddhism, Hinduism, and Catholicism in the soft light of the cabin he shared with his woman, a candlemaker he'd met after a year on the job, but withheld from her his skepticism about reincarnation and Biblical creation. "What's the good word?" his woman would coo when he'd set down yet another holy book or book about spiritual seeking. He'd look up with childlike eyes and say, "I get the foot-washing, and the vow of silence too." Aside from silence he liked the crackling fire and his woman's worn voice, and the wind and the birds in the trees by the highway.

The roadkill collector studied kosher law, and when he'd come upon a battered deer in agony he'd set a cloth beneath its head and sever its jugular with a swift, deep stroke. When he'd wash off the blood, or bits of entrails and feces from a torn-open coyote or raccoon, he'd reflect on the lives of Untouchables.

His wife had named him "The Unreachable" for his workaholic hours and the alcohol-sodden nights when he'd lapse into silence after spending his life force and all of his words bullying people in depositions. In philosophical moods he'd put his whiskey glass down and tell Janet, "I don't see you complaining about this huge house and three cars," and she'd drink and say, "Devil's bargain." Then he'd peek through the door at his daughter sleeping. He did this for years 'til she'd grown and flown, then his wife stood firm in their high-ceilinged entrance hall and declared with a sweeping gesture at the house, "You're not taking this from me."

"It's all yours," he said, and with deep remorse added, "You deserve it."

His daughter zoomed past on her way to her mother's house for winter break. She did not recognize the man kneeling to a dead deer, nor hear him consoling a mortified couple staring down at the deer. She didn't recall her father striking a deer on the road home from Tahoe when she was three, or crying about it all the way home, or her father growling at her mother that the animal was dead, god damn it, and even if it wasn't, he had court the next day.

"Relax, hon," drawls the driving instructor. "If you die, I die."

He's looking right at me, but I look straight ahead even though we're still idling in front of my house. He's one of those losers who looks about fifty when they're just thirty-two, with a face that looks like it's being sucked down a drain. And he's lighting a cigarette!

"Would you put that out, please?"

He lets out a sigh and rolls down the window and hangs his arm out. He's a poser, this loser, wearing a tight t-shirt to show off his arms even though it's cold out. His blond hair is long, and that's cool, but it's stringy and greasy, and disgusting to look it.

"*Those*'ll kill you," I say.

"Hooray," he smirks, "you got an A in health class."

I clamp my mouth shut: an A in health and everything else.

What a dumb little driving-school car! This guy's six-foot-moron and his knees are hiked up, and it's my turn to smirk. I feel him staring at my face, then my neck, and now his stare's crawling over my chest, which has developed lately. "Are we going?" I say. I'm mad at myself, 'cause my voice has just cracked.

"Whoa," he says, "first you're afraid of dying, now you can't wait to go."

"I didn't say I was afraid of dying, I'm merely concerned about whether I'm advanced enough for the freeway." *I'm merely concerned*, words straight from Mom's playbook.

"Like I said, if you die, I die."

My hands are fixed at ten and two. I stare straight ahead. "Maybe you want to die." I say this to hurt him, 'cause I think that it's true.

"Maybe," he says without hesitation.

I'm supposed to feel sorry for him.

"Not you though," he says, jerks his head at our house. It's a big house, I admit it, a white colonial with red brick. Mom's flower boxes have red and white cyclamen, and our porch has a swing and a bed for the dog. And I cry, god damn it.

"Okay, listen," he says in a deep phony voice. "Let's not go yet."

"No, let's." I floor the gas pedal and aim the right headlight straight at a lamppost five houses down.

THE WALKER

The walker did not wish to die.

The walker did not wish not to die.

The walker listened to the *Tao Te Ching* on his five-mile walks. He felt a surge of pride for his endurance at age seventy-four, then chided himself for indulging in pride, then smiled at the foolishness of chiding.

The walker walked along a strip of unkempt parkland parallel to a busy boulevard. Streets perpendicular to the boulevard poured into it. The walker crossed thirty-six of these streets each day. If a car were approaching he would freeze in the crosswalk just short of its path and seek the driver's eyes, hoping that the moral authority of a long, well lived life would induce them to stop. Sometimes they would, sometimes they'd blow past.

The walker formed Walk Safe SF when yet another pedestrian was killed by a car. He told fellow walkers that when cars were new they were compared to Moloch, the god to whom ancients sacrificed their children. As he walked he considered the briefness of life, the ugly blacktops that covered up nature, and the ugly metal hulks that killed the bird songs and severed the walkways. So unbearably, unspeakably dumb.

Lao Tzu said: He who is skillful walks the land without having to shun the rhinoceros, for in him there is no place of death.

The walker embraced this and walked with pure heart on a course that would set him before cars that must yield—by law and moral right alike. They would stop, and he'd wave. A barreling pickup didn't slow down, and the walker faced death with his arms at his sides—but the pickup swerved, hit a biker and killed him. Male, 27 (name withheld pending notification of kin).

HANNA-BARBERA

"Hanna-BAR-buhr-uh?!" Simon clown-screeched and pranced on the lunch-table bench. I sank my arms onto the puddle of milk I had spilled and didn't notice it rolling 'til my crotch turned cold. "It's not Hanna-BAR-buhr-uh, it's Hanna-bar-BEAR-uh! Like Yogi The Bear!" Then he marched back and forth in that robotic low-budget Hanna-Barbera style, moving just one arm at a time going "Hardy har har!" like the cartoon hyena, with a lunch bag as Hardy's porkpie hat. All the kids laughed with genuine mirth and also in fear that he would cut them next, for he was sharp and mean as his studio exec dad.

***

"Say *Hanna-BAR-buhr-uh*," I growl through the ski mask, and Simon, on his back, having long since replaced his aged father as studio head, looks helplessly out the window for studio security—but I'm security chief, and the two a.m. patrol has just passed. "Say it," I say, and he says it, and his pupils shrink to nothing, and he doesn't dare move as I pour a quart of cold milk on the crotch of his Armani slacks. "Tell 'em Heisenberg did this," I say, and set the porkpie on his soaking disgrace.

Picture a kill.

A high school courtyard filled with grads. Deely-boppers, rainbow wigs, Darth Vader masks, devil's ears. Bow-tied teachers mugging for pictures, slit-skirted sisters sipping from flasks. Picture me, an outcast nerd.

Picture Hammerhead Hirsch. Bookstore cowboy, minor Beat icon, long-ago Golden Gloves boxing champ. Head pictures me as a poet and dreamer, not his adoring sidekick only. Head's hair is swept back in iron-gray waves, his burly chest strains his fresh Hawaiian, his mad-merry eyes hint of wondrous knowledge the squares aren't hip to.

Picture my mother in a grey pants suit. She is as slender and straight as an aspen, and a brave smile cracks a façade hardened by a bitter divorce from a cheating husband four years before.

Picture my mom meeting Hammerhead Hirsch, whose licentious cave has been my hangout for three years. They are years, Mom believes, that I should have been home in our all-white apartment, where she fights depression by steam-cleaning the carpet three times a week.

"Your nickname is *Head*, Mr. Hirsch?" Mom's face is pinched with the strain of conversing politely with a boho.

"Yes, ma'am," says Head, dusting off his formal manners, "but it's got nothing to do with grass, I assure you–folks oft make that error. *Head*'s short for *Hammerhead*, for the way I could take a punch back in the day."

"You're a colorful man," says Mom stiffly. She looks restively around the courtyard but finds no comfort in the pulsating throng.

But she does see my father.

My well-tanned father saunters towards us like an L.A. cliché in his beige linen jacket and lime-green silk shirt with two buttons undone. His expression is that of a man who has walked into just the wrong party and needs a drink badly.

"This is my father," I tell Head.

94

My father stretches out the hand that has shaken dozens of hands of homebuyers in the affluent western end of the San Fernando Valley. "Pleased to meet you," he slurs with an insouciant grin. "I've heard *nothing* about you."

Head laughs off the gibe as the normal behavior of a stressed alpha male.

Mom stares at the alpha with naked loathing.

Picture an assassin. For years the assassin has stalked her prey but can rarely get near him. On the rare occasions when the prey is near, he is well guarded. Likewise my father is rarely near, for he ceased making the hour-plus drive from the Valley to see me shortly after Mom and I moved to Venice. And he is always well guarded–not by Secret Service agents, but by the presence of some girlfriend or other who is prettier and younger than Mom, and capable by her presence alone of disemboweling her.

Picture an assassin praying for years for one clear shot.

Picture my mother getting that shot.

Drawn by the occasion, my father has made the long drive from West Hills and entered willingly into Mom's presence. Bowing to decency, he has deposited his girlfriend at the far side of the courtyard. His very own son, whom he scarcely knows–although he casually, promiscuously says on the phone now and then that he "really ought to spend more time with you, Robbie"–has provided the ammunition to bring him down. Knowing her target will flitter off soon, my mother takes aim.

"Mr. Hirsch is quite an important figure in your son's life," she says. "Your son calls him his father figure. He says he's really his dad, in effect."

My dad's head jerks back like JFK's. The wound is mortal, there can be no doubt. The Hand That Pumped Ten-Thousand Fists lingers in Head's grasp as if my father has forgotten the simple procedure of *clasp, shake, remove*; and the face that beams from a series of Top Producer photos searches Head's face like an addled old man trying to remember who on earth this might be.

Head performs triage. "Mr. Steiner," he says, squeezing my father's hand with masculine reassurance, "your son may've called me *Daddio* once or twice out of respect for my Beat days, but that's as far as that *father* riff goes. Matter of fact, he's told me a million times that his way with words comes straight from you—and I'll tell you, sir, your honor student's got the gift of gab big-time."

My father's smile has sagged and collapsed. He grasps the shoulders of a son he scarcely knows, understanding now that he never will. His drowning eyes beg a hug of his son, but it is not to be, for the son too is drowning. The man clasps his grad's cheeks. "Just look at you," he says, groping for the right note. "You've done it, my boy." But *my boy* rings as false as a dying man's prayer upon a deathbed conversion.

I look into eyes that have shrunk to pinpoints. For the lack of anything better to do, my father sticks a hundred-dollar bill in my pocket. Seeking words but finding none, he walks away on weakening legs.

Staring after with grim satisfaction, the assassin watches her victim die.

HUNGER FOR PEACE: A MOB FAIRY TALE

All of our birthdays came in a row, and the numbers that year were rich with meaning.

I followed Scrapple's *Lucky Seven* with my own *Big Two-One*. Head gave me a coupon for five free singing lessons with himself, plus a charcoal caricature of a goateed me which a Lantern regular had drawn to illustrate one of my Head-bestowed nicknames: *Toulouse*. Head had handed me that handle years before for my role as chronicler of the scenes at The Lantern and The Fusebox, and he'd dusted it off for frequent use now because the moniker suited my new ladykiller (huh huh) Toulouse-Lautrec goatee *and* poked fun at my *too-loose* pants and *too-loose* lips, the latter a jab at a few loose quips I'd made about Head's morns abed and mounting expenses. Nevertheless it was a Hammerhead name, and I treasured it thusly.

Head's own big-numbered birthday, his *Big Five-Oh*, came the first week of June. It was, he said, a meaningless number. But as numbers go, it was big and round and momentous enough, in my mind at least, to warrant an extra-special gift, which I bought for Head with a full week's pay–a VCR, his first ever.

Head held the unit in the big loving hands that had held Baby Bookmark. "Can you set it up, dude?" If there was one thing I knew, it was home entertainment–and Head's intimate *dude* reflected my increased importance in his life. As I set the unit up, Scrapple ran circles around me whooping like a worshipful primitive, and Head trekked into the garage and returned with a head full of dust and a videotape in hand. "I've been waiting to play this forever, dude." He nodded at the unit as if he himself were unworthy to touch it. I inserted the tape, and Head said with misty-eyes directed more to spirits in the air than to me, "J.T.'s antiwar mob film, *Hunger for Peace: A Mob Fairy Tale.* Jer financed it himself in the thick of the Cold War."

We settled onto the couch as if at a premiere. The plot unfolded in the familiar way. A big-city mob rises to power. A crosstown mob encroaches on its turf, and first blood is spilled. In a departure from form, a midget and a zombie hit man figure in the gunplay—"experimental" said Head in a cineaste hush—and the prospect of an all-out turf war arises. The mobs parlay at a smoke-filled Italian restaurant, the chieftains flanked by flinty-mugged toughs. One is Head, a pug-nosed young heavy in a sharp-lapelled suit, a slanted fedora, a charcoal shirt, and a stiletto tie. The plot veers radically off-course at this point as the leaders decide to make peace, not war.

"Now comes a real-time dinner to celebrate the peace," Head said with eyes riveted to the screen. "With the dinner dialogue all improvised. Daring stuff."

"*It seems to me*," improvises one mob boss, wiping his lips after finishing a luscious antipasto, "*we could use more prosciutto.*"

A murderous silence ensues, broken at length by the boss of Head's mob. "*I think we'll be fine without the prosciutto, Eddie... Don Eddie. You know, the minestrone is nice.*"

A terrible pause and a shifting of eyes as the gunmen look around, wondering whether the newly-made peace is about to be shattered. The actors, a hodgepodge of J.T.'s flamboyant gay friends and young Warhol-worshipping actors from the Tickler's wait staff, shift uneasily on their feet as they wonder who among them will improvise a resolution to the unexpected plot crisis. Suddenly Head puts his fingers and thumb together Italian style, inclines his head towards the middle of the table, leans slightly towards the dons and says, in his best Brando hush: "*I'll be happy to get some more prosciutto, Don Eddie. No problem.*"

"J.T. said that line made the film," glowed Head. "Look, here comes the disarmament scene." The waiter, a gay actor, sashays around the table collecting guns and stilettos which the heavies obediently place on his tray. "*You know,*" Don Eddie says to murmurs of approval from the now-enlightened thugs, "*with all the moolah we will save by not buying guns, we can build a few schools... and maybe a park!*" Ah, but the mobs have one last fight left in them—they fight over the check. The credits roll to "Where Have All the Flowers Gone"—sung by Head, in convincing Italian—and the credits conclude with a dedication: "*To*

Daniel Ellsberg, who had the guts to expose the madness. Il fin?"

Scrap jumped up shouting, "Dad was a star in the movies, oh yeah!" Lenny batted Howie around, and Scrap jumped down from the couch onto the dogpile like Stone Cold Steve Austin, his wrestling fave.

"Awesome," I said, by which I meant–*awesome*. "But what was with the zombie hit man?"

My question snapped Head out of his reverie. "Hell, I don't remember, it stood for something." But his perturbation was fleeting, for he hooked my neck with his elbow and planted a smack atop my head like the kiss of death.

THE IDLE INTELLECTUALS SIP AND SUP

The three members of The Idle Intellectuals Sipping & Sustenance Society agreed on one thing beside Café Salon's French-press Toscano:

"Humility," observed Sims, his scone held aloft like the light of truth, "is the natural state of the mature intellect."

"Precisely," said Sam. "As Aristotle said, 'It is the mark of an educated man to be able to entertain a thought without accepting it.'"

"Or educated woman," chided Juno, sucking jam from a long slender finger and air-marking "one point."

Sam reclaimed the finger and wiped it clean. "Ari wouldn't have had any female students, but fair point."

"Irrelevant," said Sims, "it was 'educated *mind*.' Incidentally, Plato may have inspired Aristotle with his own famed quotation, 'The only thing I know is that I know nothing.'"

"Not likely," said Juno, "since Socrates said that."

"Don't mess with a Greek on the subject of Greeks!" said Sam, reaching a high-five to Juno.

"I'm Croatian," said Juno, eluding Sam's hand. "They renamed the grandfolks *Vazakis* at Immigration because they couldn't understand *Vukasovic*."

"Interesting," said Sam. "But to back up a step, we can't be sure Socrates even said that at all, because he hated writing and railed against it. So who knows if it was even written down?"

"Accuracy of reporting must always be questioned," mused Sims. "As Yogi said, 'I never said half of the things I said.'"

Juno sighed, "I love Yogi Berra as much as anyone, but I've always suspected that of being a phony quotation invented to serve as a book title."

"It does seem to lack the essential quality of Yogi's bona fide malaprops," Sam reflected, "inherent good sense betrayed by weird syntax."

Mused Sims, "Financial considerations often mar truth."

"As do political considerations," added Juno. "Didn't it ever occur to you that Socrates' profession of ignorance could have been a pose to sandbag the Athenian rulers who charged him with corrupting youth?"

"Plausible," said Sam. "But I've heard that the quotation is a mistranslation of 'The only thing I know is that *our leaders* know nothing.'"

"Really?" said the others, agog.

"No," grinned Sam. "Played you."

"Samantha Chang," said Juno, "you are a menace! Omigod! Look at Sims!"

Sims' head had exploded in response to Sam's jest, and the dozens of green and blue superballs that had sprung from his skull were bouncing wildly about the café.

"Uncool!" cried Bob, who was role-playing Sims. "We were still in Level One Reality! You're making a mockery of our quest for truth!"

"This game's making a mockery of my day," said Iris, playing Juno. "Three hours' of Epistemo on the nicest Saturday of the year is for the birds!" She tossed the controller onto Bob's messy bed, dove out of the third-floor window, and flew up into a cottony sky. But a sudden wind hurled her down towards the earth,

which awakend the dreamer,
a woman named Zoe,
from what had been a lovely sleep

evidently.

– the end –

By Marquez Dalí
(not)

APOLLO'S LIGHT

Golden youth,
Raise clear river-water
To Delphic height!
Disdain to honor as daylight, night!

"A bit sweet, perhaps?" Aristokles glowed with the light of Apollo: So thought his novice, a youthful paragon.

"It likes us," said Philon, pressing the master-priest's hand to his cheek.

"Well," said the master. "The Oracle has spoken then."

Her disjointed mutterings refined and augmented by the master and transcribed by the novice, the stupefied oracle fixed the beauteous youth with the gaze of she who moves earth, sea, and sky. The bewitched youth lacked the art to dissemble, and the Pythia's smile glowed like moonlight.

The master bodily turned the youth from the Oracle. He himself forebore looking at the young woman, though two years before he had gazed at her dancing wildly in a wood. Swiftly had he arranged her ordination, then shared with her pleasures of body and mind. But now she was restless, and he filled with dread.

At the portal he addressed the novice. "May Apollo approve your efforts at the Nemean Games! May our creed guard your honor: *Nothing in excess.*"

The youth's smile reflected the master's enlightened glow. "Thrive Apollo! May Dionysos perish unvenerated!"

The master's gaze followed the well-loved youth's path down to the plain; then he attended the messenger of an Athenian sea-trader contemplating a venture.

In his chamber he wrote:

Go! Do not fear Poseidon's fury

He dispatched the messenger and sought out the Pythia in her

102

sanctum. Apollo's rays deepened the lineaments in the man's brow; the Pythia apprehended his dread. She cupped a bowl of wine in soft hands and held it to his lips. At times the libation roused Eros; presently it opened a course to the man's heart.

"I never knew woman before you, love!" He knelt at her feet, settled his anguished brow on her lap.

"Foolish cult, to geld great men! I drink to Dionysos!" She stroked his hoary hair, shared sweet consoling love with the man.

The youth, crowned in celery-leaves, burst into the master's chamber three weeks hence. The Oracle slumbered in the master's arms amidst lyre, flute, figs, and wine. "Profaners!" the youth gasped.

A thunderhead railed, lightning bolts clove mountains, Poseidon's tempest capsized a rich fleet.

The ruined sea-trader set the fateful message before the priesthood. "It says, *'Go! Do not fear Poseidon's fury'*!"

The master priest examined the transcription:

"'Go! Do not fear Poseidon's fury' ... was written!

'Go do not! Fear Poseidon's fury' ... was spoken!

"Our novitiate–Oh! That sacred duty compels us to speak true! – Erred in transcribing the Oracle's word–is proven blind to Apollo's light."

Swift as Hermes the wailing youth fled, to return to lofty Delphi no more.

STILL LIFE WITH TONGS

Stillness reigned in the chamber: the suspect, naked, chin crusted with blood, lay limply upon the wooden frame; the black-hooded torturer clutched his tongs; the black-robed inquisitor stood with hands clasped, prepared at a word to offer God's mercy.

"My son," the inquisitor said through tight lips, "confess the Jewish devil within."

The suspect studied the inquisitor through blood-engorged eyes. His features were those of Rebekah's father, who had fled to Morocco when Granada fell. Perhaps the rumors were true after all, that the inquisitor was descended from Jews.

The inquisitor grimaced. Who was this loathsome Jew to stare? And he surely was a Jew, despite his denial. And yet... there was doubt. True, a neighbor had seen him feeding pork to his dog, pork that he claimed to have bought for his table. True, neighbors had heard mournful Hebraic prayers emanating from his home on a Friday night. But his features weren't Jewish, the inquisitor felt, and he had exposed hundreds of Marranos.

The suspect stared at the inquisitor, who shuddered with revulsion at a gaze that presumed to penetrate him—with wonder first, then with pity. Pity from a heretical dog!

The inquisitor's expression reminded the suspect of Rebekah's revulsion when he touched a consoling hand to her shoulder. Every day she prayed at home for Moshe, the unborn child she had miscarried during her stay in the dungeon; in church every day she prayed for "Pedro." Rebekah and the suspect had shared such love that he had secretly converted to Judaism for her. But that love had died, and she was a stranger.

"Admit you're a Jew," said the inquisitor. "Confess and be free."

"I confess," the suspect muttered through grotesque swollen lips, his words whistling through the gaps in his teeth. "I confess myself more Christlike than you." The inquisitor snapped his head back. The suspect took aim with a deadly dart. "And I'm more Jewish, too. Surely you remember that Christ was a Jew."

"Blasphemer! Cur!" The inquisitor drew from a deep well of power to compose himself. "However," he said, bending to the man's ear, "I shall be pleased to strengthen you in your claim."

He pointed at the torture implements on a table.

The torturer grabbed two spikes and the hammer.

"Miss MacDermott's enormous blueberry eyes may well have evolved on the gloomy moors of Scotland to maximize the reception of light."

The young teacher's words were meant to awaken a seventeen-year-old mind; they awakened more.

"*Suh*," said the girl's alarmed beau with a comic burlesque of his small town drawl, "are you sayin' we came from *monkihs*... with *blue aahs*?" His football pals chortled with the impunity of youth on the last day of school.

Mr. Dupree's lonely summer was dominated by the Scopes trial and enlivened by Latin lessons that he gave in his modest boarding house room. Miss McDermott gazed dreamily as he recited Horace. Shortly before school was to resume, she reached for the lemonade and brushed the man's hand. He knocked over the pitcher and ended the lessons.

"I repeat," Mr. Dupree said after class, alone with Miss McDermott and her boyfriend, as if taking the Fifth, "the teaching of evolution has been banned in this state. So let's stick to mitosis."

"But Mr. Dupree," said the girl, "it's just us here. And evolution *is* right, isn't it?"

Mr. Dupree looked into the girl's wide-opened eyes and those of her beau—an innocent boy despite all his blather. "Well," the teacher chuckled, "the presence of the KKK on the hallowed ground of the nation's capital may suggest otherwise—but, yes, evolution is right."

Gratified smiles played on young faces.

After enclosing the letter to the school board, Miss MacDermott slid a pink tongue across the seal and gazed at her beau with sparkling eyes like dew-dropped blueberries.

INSIDIOUS

"You, Rosie, are... " The sky over the beach was as unlimited as we youthful American rulers of the world. My handsome warrior raised his eyes to that bountiful sky and plucked the right words for a girl like me. "You're as sweet and lush as tropical fruit."

A girl like me is no dummy. I'd earned straight As in high school, I'd supervised a squad of Red Cross volunteers, and at age twenty-one I'd finally accepted Aunt Mildred's advice that I "show more cleavage and less brains"–thus this lovely swimsuit with the brazen halter top. I'd even seen *Insidious*, that Hitchcock film about a roguish charmer. Nevertheless.

"You're a romantic, Charlie."

Charlie's face was golden from two months on the beach, and I basked in the glow; but something primal in his smile broke my gaze, and I found myself staring at the stump where his toe used to be.

"Iwo Jima," he muttered. "What the hell is a toe with all that I've seen?" He withdrew deep inside himself to contemplate horrors far worse than we girls on the homefront had viewed every week in sanitized newsreels in air-conditioned theaters.

I touched his hand with the magic touch of a fairy, for he returned to the present wearing a broad smile. "I think of this–" he waved at the pristine white sand, multi-colored umbrellas, bathers carousing, a little girl dripping ice cream– "and I think of the beaches on Iwo Jima, Tarawa..." Again he was gone.

"Hush," I assured him, "there's no need to talk," and I shared a first kiss that offered much more.

1946. A war had just ended. Now it's 1967, and a terrible new war is raging in Asia. I received precious little from my hit-and-run warrior in exchange for my all on that warm afternoon–little aside from the love of my life, my twenty year-old son–but I did receive a valuable lesson when I finally learned the truth.

A toe, dear boy, is a small price to pay to stay out of a war.

Tomorrow we cut.

ABOUT THE AUTHOR

Jon Sindell prefers to let his fiction define him.

If you are reading this, however, you deserve more. Therefore ...

Jon is a Los Angeles native who moved permanently to San Francisco in the early Eighties.

Jon has a wife and kids, a dog and cats. He does his best by them. They forgive him his failings.

Jon is a longtime vegetarian, a home cook, a gardener, and a hiker.

What is Jon else? Wait, there's no need to go quoting Shakespeare around here!

Though Jon does love Shakespeare. He also holds J.D. Salinger, Tobias Wolff, Kazuo Ishiguro, Mark Twain, F. Scott Fitzgerald, and Raymond Carver in the highest regard.

Jon practiced law for twenty years, but has earned his bread for the past ten years as a fulltime personal tutor of students from middle school through grad school in English literature and writing, history, government, creative thinking and critical thinking, and as a writing coach for business professionals. He can't believe how great his second career is.

Jon is the author of the baseball–plus novel *The Mighty Roman Baseball Blast*, a fast, funny story about baseball and the modern American man.

His short fiction has appeared in about seventy magazines.

Jon began writing flash fiction intensively in 2013. *The Roadkill Collection* is his first collection. He is enormously grateful to Big Table Publishing for believing in his work.

Jon writes fiction of every length, and has just discovered, to his surprise, that writing an author bio is not the worst ordeal ever. He would, however, like to disappear once again into the background of new stories.

Therefore, Dear Reader, he bids you farewell with heartfelt gratitude.